Spelunking Scripture:
Christmas

Exploring Important Passages of the Bible

BRUCE C. SALMON

© 2021
Published in the United States by Nurturing Faith, Macon, GA.
Nurturing Faith is a book imprint of Good Faith Media (goodfaithmedia.org).
Library of Congress Cataloging-in-Publication Data is available.

ISBN: 978-1-63528-147-7

All scripture citations are from the New Revised International Version (NRSV)
unless otherwise indicated.

Contents

Introduction

Christmas is a big deal—in our culture, in our families, and in our churches. The Christmas season is the most popular holiday of the year. Almost everyone knows about the baby in the manger, except that in some circles, Santa Claus is more popular than Jesus. Still, the Christmas story is largely known. Why then a study of the scripture passages that tell the Christmas story? Is "spelunking scripture" necessary for Christmas? I contend the answer is "yes," because many people never get beneath the surface of the Christmas story. The basic details may be known, but the deeper meaning of the Christmas story may be undiscovered. That is the purpose of this study—to go beneath the surface of the story to discover what Christmas really means.

You might know that the early Christians did not celebrate Christmas. They knew of the accounts in Matthew and Luke about the birth of Jesus, but their focus was on his death and resurrection, not his nativity. According to Hans Hillerbrand, professor emeritus of history and religion at Duke University, "the actual observance of the day of Jesus' birth was long in coming. In particular, during the first two centuries of Christianity, there was strong opposition to recognizing birthdays of martyrs, or, for that matter, of Jesus."[1] The early Church Fathers considered celebrating birthdays a pagan custom. Saints and martyrs were honored on the days of their martyrdom, which were considered their true "birthdays."

We are not sure how December 25 became the date of Jesus' birth. It may have been connected with a popular Roman holiday that celebrated the winter solstice. The first "Christ Mass" in the Roman Catholic Church occurred centuries later, and many of the other Christmas traditions developed over time. The Puritans in colonial New England resisted celebrating Christmas altogether, because the custom of exchanging Christmas gifts between family members and friends had secular overtones.

The story of the birth of Jesus is absent in Mark's gospel, and is only alluded to in the prologue to John's gospel. Matthew began his nativity story with the genealogy of Jesus and the surprising revelation that his mother Mary was with child from the Holy Spirit, before she and Joseph were married. The actual birth of Jesus is described in Matthew in a single verse (1:25). It is Luke's gospel that fills in the details about the angelic annunciation to Mary, her "Magnificat" response, the trip to Bethlehem, the birth in a barnyard, laying the baby in a manger because (as the Christmas carol says) there was "no crib for a bed," the angelic annunciation to the shepherds, and the shepherds' going with haste to find Mary and Joseph and the child.

Not surprisingly, most of the focus in spelunking Christmas is on Luke's gospel, although Matthew's brief account of Jesus' birth and the subsequent visit of the wise men is often included in the story. Also, the prophecy from Isaiah 9 about a child being born for us is included, especially since it was put to music in Handel's *Messiah*. Finally, the prologue to John's gospel about the Word being made flesh and living among us provides a theological underpinning to the Christmas story.

The methodology of spelunking scripture is to briefly introduce each pertinent scripture passage related to the Christmas story, and then to illustrate each passage with studies gleaned from sermons that seek to make a connection between the text and life today. Needless to say, as a pastor who served the same church for 33 years, I preached on the various Christmas passages many times. Do the math: With four Sundays in Advent, and the candlelight service on Christmas Eve, and Epiphany Sunday, I had many opportunities to explore what the Christmas story might mean for us. Yet, even though the Christmas story was well known to most people in my congregation, there was always something "new" to say, because the story continues to speak to the changing contexts of our lives.[2]

This study is part of the Bible study series *Spelunking Scripture*. Other individual volumes will explore passages from the Gospels (not including the nativity and resurrection stories), the letters of Paul, the Acts of the Apostles and the general epistles of the New Testament, and the Old Testament. There is also *Spelunking Scripture—Easter*, which will explore the accounts of the resurrection in the Gospels. The current volume explores passages from Isaiah, Matthew, Luke, and John related to the birth of Jesus.

Almost everyone in our culture knows about Christmas, but do we know what Christmas means? Let us explore together these important scripture passages to move beneath the surface to the underlying messages for our lives.

NOTES

[1] Hans J. Hillerbrand's quote comes from www.brittanica.com/topic/Christmas.
[2] Each study for a given passage contains both new insights and familiar commentary.

CHAPTER 1

FOR UNTO US A CHILD IS BORN

(Isa. 9:1-7)

The people walking in darkness have seen a great light. On those living in a pitch-dark land, light has dawned. A child is born to us, a son is given to us, and authority will be on his shoulders. He will be named Wonderful Counselor, Mighty God, Eternal Father, Prince of Peace.

(Isa. 9:2, 6 CEB)

"For unto us a child is born." So begins the chorus in Handel's magnificent oratorio, *Messiah*. Although Isaiah, writing in the 8th century BC, did not specify who that child was, we know that he was prophesying about Jesus. Isaiah was envisioning a messianic king who would establish endless peace for "David's throne and his kingdom, establishing and sustaining it with justice and righteousness, now and forever" (Isa. 9:7).

Isaiah's message of hope was delivered to Jerusalem and the southern kingdom of Judah at a time when the northern kingdom of Israel had been conquered and annexed into the empire of Assyria. Isaiah identified this messianic king as a shoot from the stump of Jesse (King David's father), and one on whom the spirit of the Lord shall rest (11:1-2). In his opening genealogy, Matthew connected the dots, tracing the lineage of Jesus Christ through his earthly father Joseph all the way back to King David and to Jesse and ultimately to Abraham (1:1-17). It was as if Matthew wanted to show that Jesus fulfilled the prophesy of the messianic king given by Isaiah almost eight centuries before.

Jesus had many names. The angel told Joseph in a dream that Mary would bear a son conceived of the Holy Spirit. Joseph was to name him Jesus, for he would save his people from their sins. The name Jesus comes from a Hebrew word meaning "savior." Jesus also would be called Messiah (from the Hebrew) and Christ (from the Greek). Both names mean "anointed one." Jesus also would be called Emmanuel, which means "God is with us." This name came from a prophecy in Isaiah 7:14. Another prophecy in Isaiah said he would be called "Wonderful Counselor, Mighty God, Everlasting Father, Prince of Peace" (9:6).

So, Jesus had many names, because one name was not enough to describe who he was. Jesus was all those names, and more. He was Jesus of Nazareth, Rabbi, Lord, Savior, Messiah, Christ. He was Emmanuel; he was "God with us." He was "Wonderful Counselor, Mighty God, Everlasting Father, Prince of Peace." He was Son of David (Matt. 9:27, 15:22), Son of God, Son of Man. He was the Human One (CEB). He was the Word made flesh. He was God the only Son, who was close to the Father's heart (John 1:18).

POKING HOLES IN THE DARKNESS
(Isa. 9:2-7)

Perhaps you remember the author, Robert Louis Stevenson, who wrote the classic novels *Treasure Island, Kidnapped,* and *The Strange Case of Dr. Jekyll and Mr. Hyde.* What you may not know is that Robert Louis Stevenson had to overcome many obstacles in his life. He suffered almost continuous poor health. As a boy, he was so sickly that he was out of school more than he was in, yet he was able to enter Edinburgh University at the age of 16. As a man, he suffered frequent bouts of illness, but he kept on writing. Finally, he spent the last years of his life in the South Seas, where he died of a cerebral hemorrhage at the age of 44.

One evening as a boy, Stevenson was at his home in Scotland, sick in bed. His nurse came into his bedroom and found him with his nose pressed against the frosty window. "Child, come away from there," she said. "You'll catch your death of cold." But young Robert Louis would not move. He sat there, transfixed, gazing out the window at a lamplighter who was working his way down the street. He watched the old man stop at each street lamp and light it with the flame on his pole, and then move on to the next street lamp and light it, and then the next, leaving a trail of tiny lights behind. Pointing at the lamplighter Robert exclaimed: "Look there; that man is poking holes in the darkness!"[1]

It was a dark time when Isaiah gave his prophecy in our scripture passage. Obviously, it was physically dark then, with no streetlights of any kind, but it was dark from a spiritual standpoint too. It was a time of war, when the Assyrian armies were rampaging through the northern kingdom of Israel and threatening the southern kingdom of Judah. The merciless Assyrian king, Tiglath-Pileser, had the Hebrew people scared out of their wits at what might happen to them. They feared for their lives, and for their continued existence as a people. In the midst of this dark and fearsome time, Isaiah gave his incredibly optimistic prophecy of hope, saying "The people walking in darkness have seen a great light. On those living in a pitch-dark land, light has dawned."

Looking into the future, Isaiah was convinced that the dark time surrounding his people would pass. He was convinced that God would prevail against the darkness and deliver his people from fear and death. Isaiah pictured a time of rejoicing, when the people would celebrate as they did at the harvest, or when the army returned home victorious from war. He recalled the time, hundreds of years before, when Gideon led a small band against the Midianites, and by God's hand removed the threat of Midian. Isaiah foresaw a time when the instruments of war would be burned for fuel and the people would live in justice and perpetual peace. All this would take place because the Lord would give a son, a child, a king, to deliver his people and lift them to a higher level of living. This son, this child, this king, would be called "Wonderful Counselor, Mighty God, Eternal Father, Prince of Peace."

Looking back at Jewish history, we know that such events never happened in Isaiah's time. In fact, it would be another 700 years until this prophecy would be fulfilled, and even then, not everyone would recognize it when it happened. The people were expecting an earthly king to deliver them, a mighty warrior, a fighter similar to King David.

Instead, God sent a different kind of king, a different kind of child, a different kind of son, to save his people. When a baby was born in a stable in Bethlehem, who could have guessed that he would be the one Isaiah had foreseen so long ago? But now we know that Jesus was the promised one whom God sent to poke holes in the darkness, to be the light of the world. Now we know that Jesus was the son Isaiah talked about, who would be called Wonderful Counselor, Mighty God, Eternal Father, Prince of Peace. Jesus came to be the light of the world. And yet, more than two thousand years after his coming, the world is still a dark and fearsome place.

It was one of the most tragic events I can remember as a pastor. Our entire community was rocked by a senseless act of violence at the Washington, D.C. police headquarters. An ex-con with a record of drugs and weapons charges burst in and began firing a semi-automatic handgun. Before he turned the gun on himself, he killed three people—a D.C. police officer and two FBI agents. One of the agents killed was the son-in-law of one of our most active church members. Mike Miller and his wife and their two young children had worshipped at our church. Mike was gunned down while he was working on unsolved murder cases. If you want a picture of the kind of darkness Isaiah was talking about, you need look no further than what happened to Mike Miller and the two officers at the D.C. police headquarters.

At the time when Mike was murdered, I was serving on the grand jury for Prince George's County in suburban Maryland, adjacent to Washington, D.C. When I first was summoned to grand jury duty, the jury coordinator told me that I would be exposed to a side of life in our community that I could hardly believe. She was right. Grand jurors are not permitted to discuss any cases, but I can tell you in general terms what you might already know from watching the news on television. Our society is drowning in a sea of violence and illegal drug trafficking. There are so many crimes going on that two grand juries would convene every week to handle all the indictments. One grand jury handled only narcotics, murders, and police shootings. The other grand jury handled the remaining crimes.

The threat to our society is not from without but from within. It is not the Assyrian army camped on our borders that we worry about. It is the moral decline within our communities that threatens to engulf our society in darkness. What is the reason for all the violence and drugs? There is a shocking disregard for human life. We are talking about the power of evil taking root in human hearts, a spiritual darkness that can only be overcome by spiritual light.

The world was a dark place in Isaiah's time, it was a dark place when Jesus was born, and it is still a dark place today. The problem is not the Light. The problem is with those who are called to bear witness to the Light. We have not done enough to poke holes in the darkness.

Mike Miller, the FBI agent who had attended our church and who was murdered at the D.C. police headquarters, was not an outwardly religious person, but he operated out of religious convictions. He believed he was called to make a difference, and he invested his life in making the world a better place. At one point, he left the FBI because the long hours conflicted with his family responsibilities. He went back to practicing law, and he probably could have made a comfortable living doing that. But being a lawyer in private practice could not accomplish what he could do in law enforcement. So, he joined the FBI a second time, and he volunteered for the "Cold Cases" Special Assignment Task Force. It must have been frustrating work, and it was dangerous. But Mike knew there were hurting families out there who had lost a loved one and were waiting for justice to be done. And so, he poured himself into trying to solve those cold cases, and to bring those families some justice, and to rid society of murderers who might kill again.

Mike Miller was also a volunteer soccer, baseball, and basketball coach. Even before he had children of his own, Mike was a coach for the Boys and Girls Club. He wanted to keep those young people out of trouble; he wanted to teach them the right values in life. When we had his funeral at our church, so many people came that the FBI had to set up remote televised viewing at the church next door. Dozens of children and young people on the teams he had coached came to his funeral to show their gratitude for the example he had set for them. If Robert Louis Stevenson had been there, he would have said about Mike Miller: "Look, that man was poking holes in the darkness." Mike died as he lived, giving himself in service to others.

What about us? Maybe God has not called us to service in the FBI, but God has called us to do something about the dark places where we live. God's Light has come into our lives. For what purpose? To become lamplighters for God! We can make a difference. We can poke holes in the darkness. We can give of ourselves to help others. The torch has fallen, but the Light has not gone out. Who will pick it up to carry on?

A PROPHET'S HOPE
(Isa. 9:1-7)

What keeps a person going when others have given up? Abraham Lincoln knew something about going on in the face of adversity. He had more than his share of disappointments, setbacks, and heartaches. These are just a few of the events in Lincoln's life:

1831—experiences business failure
1832—defeated for the Illinois General Assembly
1833—endures business failure
1834—elected to the Illinois General Assembly
1835—loses fiancée to death
1836—suffers mental breakdown
1838—defeated as speaker of the Illinois General Assembly
1840—defeated as a presidential elector
1843—defeated as commissioner of the Lands Office
1843—defeated for U.S. House of Representatives
1846—elected to U.S. House of Representatives
1848—defeated for Congress
1855—defeated for the U.S. Senate
1856—defeated as U.S. vice president
1858—defeated for the U.S. Senate
1860—elected U.S. president

If you want to know something about a person's character, don't look at the successes. Rather, look at the failures. Look at what that person had to overcome. Here are some more examples of people who kept going in the face of failure:

- Admiral Peary failed on seven different attempts to reach the North Pole before he finally made it on number eight.
- Thomas Edison tried 1,600 different materials as the filament for his electric light bulb before he found the right one.
- Willie Mays did not get a hit in his first 26 times at bat in the Major League. On his 27th trip to the plate, however, as he faced pitcher Warren Spahn, he hit a home run.

What is it that keeps some people going when others have given up? Ask Isaiah. He knew something about hardships and adversity. He knew his share of disappointments and failures, both personally and as a citizen of the kingdom of Judah. Isaiah lived during a difficult time for the Jewish people. When everyone around him was caving in to fear and despair, he remained a beacon of confidence and encouragement.

What is it that keeps a person going when things are going wrong? According to the prophet, it is something called "hope." Isaiah discovered that people can endure almost anything, as long as they have hope. And this prophecy from Isaiah 9 is one of the most hope-filled passages in the Bible.

Judging by the outward circumstances of his day, Isaiah had no reason to give a prophecy like this. Times were bad in the land of Judah—very bad. A couple of hundred years before Isaiah, the Hebrew people had divided into two nations: the northern kingdom of Israel and the southern kingdom of Judah. After the division, things were not good for either kingdom. Long gone were the glory days of King David and King Solomon. After the division, each kingdom was internally wracked by scandals, political corruption, and religious idolatry. And, each kingdom was threatened by external forces. They were surrounded by hostile armies—Egypt to the south, Syria to the north, Assyria to the east. In addition, the moral climate was going down. True worship of God was becoming more and more sporadic.

During this era of two Jewish kingdoms, a series of prophets tried to call the people back to their spiritual roots. In the north, it was prophets such as Amos and Hosea. In the south, Isaiah, Micah, Jeremiah, and others tried to stem this moral decline. But by and large, the people would not listen, and things grew worse.

We are not sure exactly when Isaiah gave the prophecy in chapter 9, but perhaps it was during or just after the reign of King Ahaz in Judah. Ahaz was one of the worst kings Judah ever had. He had no scruples, no backbone, no integrity, no hint of moral leadership. The nation of Assyria, located in what is now Iraq, began to threaten the entire region. Instead of joining forces with his Hebrew brothers in the north to oppose the Assyrians, Ahaz sold out to the enemy. He encouraged the Assyrians to attack Israel! He betrayed fellow Jews. The price for this treachery was that Judah became a vassal state of the Assyrians. In addition, Ahaz replaced the true worship of God with the worship of Assyrian gods. He tore down the altars to the true God and replaced them with Assyrian altars to gods. He set up idols in the Temple. Ahaz went so far to as to burn his own sons on the foreign altars as offerings to those pagan idols. We are talking about child sacrifice! This is the kind of situation Isaiah faced.

Things were even worse in the north. The Assyrian king, Tiglath-Pileser, marched his armies into Israel and devasted the land. According to Isaiah 9:1, the lands of Zebulun and Naphtali were cursed. These were the two most northern regions of Israel, and the first ones to fall to the Assyrians. The conquest exacted a terrible toll. Many of the men were slaughtered, the women and children were carried off into captivity, and the countryside was laid waste. You can be sure that the people of Judah heard about what had happened to their cousins up north, and they began to wonder if they would be next. Tiglath-Pileser was a powerful and terrifying warrior, a barbarian with no compassion for his enemies. And with that lily-livered, two-faced, no-good Ahaz as their king, they probably felt as if they didn't have a chance to survive. This is the situation into which Isaiah gave this prophecy.

Judah was being threatened with annihilation, both internally and externally. King Ahaz was destroying the society from within, with pagan idolatry, child sacrifice, political corruption, religious perversion, and moral degradation. The Assyrian army was moving down from the north, where Israel already lay in ruins. Yet, in the midst of this terrible national crisis, Isaiah spoke these words of incredible optimism and hope: "The people walking in darkness have seen a great light. On those living in a pitch-dark land, light has dawned."

What made Isaiah say that? What made him believe that things could turn around? Every sign was that things could only get worse. What hope did the people of Judah have? What hope could Isaiah possibly offer? Just this: "A child is born to us, a son is given to us, and authority will be on his shoulders. He will be named Wonderful Counselor, Mighty God, Eternal Father, Prince of Peace." In other words, the promised child, the son, would be everything that Ahaz was not. He would be a wise leader and advisor (Wonderful Counselor). He would be a person with the power of God himself (Mighty God). He would always care for his people (Eternal Father). He would bring perpetual peace and harmony to the people (Prince of Peace).

Who was Isaiah talking about? Some commentators say he must have been talking about Hezekiah, the son of Ahaz who became king after him. Hezekiah was a good king, much better than his father, but even Hezekiah was not all that. Other scholars believe that this prophecy referred to the future king Josiah, who also was much better. Still, even Josiah came up short of those standards.

Who was Isaiah talking about? In the New Testament, Matthew gave the answer:

He left Nazareth and settled in Capernaum, which lies alongside the sea in the area of Zebulun and Naphtali. This fulfilled what Isaiah the prophet said: Land of Zebulun and land of Naphtali, alongside the sea, across the Jordan, Galilee of the Gentiles, the people who lived in the dark have seen a great light, and a light has come upon those who lived in the region and in shadow of death. (4:13-16, CEB)

It was 700 years after Isaiah before the prophecy was fulfilled. The Wonderful Counselor, the Mighty God, the Eternal Father, the Prince of Peace had a human face after all.

How did Isaiah know that Jesus was coming? How could he anticipate a messiah so many years into the future?

Isaiah had what all persons of vision have: hope. Faith in God gives that to a person. Faith in God fills us with hope. Faith in God helps us to see beyond the immediate and the temporary. Faith in God enables us to face the uncertain future with confidence and unafraid. Faith in God gives us the patience and the perseverance to endure adversity, to pass through threats and trials, to bounce back from failures, to keep going in times of darkness. Faith in God fills us with hope.

Some years ago I saw an exhibit at the National Gallery of Art in Washington, D.C. It was a showing of "Masterpieces from the Van Gogh Museum, Amsterdam." Vincent Van Gogh had managed to go on in the face of incredible adversity. Although he did not begin to paint seriously until the last 10 years of his life, having spent four of those years learning technique, during his last six years he produced an amazing collection of artistic works. Also, during those six years, Van Gogh was tormented by poor physical and mental health, financial and relationship problems, isolation, and loneliness. Yet, he produced during that time some 700 drawings and 800 oil paintings. In the final months of his life, he created an astonishing 70 paintings in 70 days. Even more remarkable is that he worked in almost absolute obscurity.

Van Gogh's name was virtually unknown outside a small circle of fellow painters. Only one article was written about him during his lifetime. He sold a grand total of one painting his entire life, and that for five francs. He was perpetually poor, supported only by small gifts from his younger brother. Spurned by the woman he loved, he was in and out of mental institutions, and in the end, at the age of 37, he took his own life. Still, today, Vincent Van Gogh is considered one of the greatest and most revolutionary Dutch painters of all time.

What kept Vincent Van Gogh going in spite of all the failures in his life? This is what he wrote to describe his art: "I want to paint men and women with that something of the eternal which the halo used to symbolize . . . to express hope by some star, the eagerness of a soul by a sunset radiance."[2] Van Gogh never was able to fulfill his dream completely, for he died a troubled and broken man. But if you will look at his paintings, you will see something of what he was seeking.

What Van Gogh could not accomplish with oils on canvas, God accomplished on the canvas of a human life. In Jesus Christ, God painted something of the eternal. In Jesus Christ, God expressed hope by a star and filled the sky of human history with the sunset radiance of his love.

Wonderful Counselor—He will guide us through life with all the wisdom we require.
Mighty God—He will fill us with the strength and power we need to get through each day.
Eternal Father—He will care about us and care for us no matter what happens.
Prince of Peace—He will fill our lives with peace—peace with God, peace with each other, peace within ourselves.

The prophet's hope is our reality. We have more than enough hope to keep going, no matter how dark our situation gets. "The people walking in darkness have seen a great light." Can you see it? Even now, the light is shining on you.

WONDERFUL
(Isa. 9:6)

The year was 1955. Christmas fell on a Sunday that year. A woman named Audrey Mieir was attending a Christmas program at a small church in Duarte, California. It was the usual pageant of days gone by—little boys dressed in bathrobes as shepherds, a teenaged girl clutching a plastic baby-doll, a grinning angel with a crooked halo waving at her parents in the second pew. The choir finished singing about sleeping in heavenly peace. Then the pastor addressed the tiny congregation. His text was Isaiah 9:6. Reading from the King James Version of the Bible, he said: "For unto us a child is born, unto us a son a given: and the government shall be upon his shoulder: and his name shall be called Wonderful, Counselor, the mighty God, the everlasting Father, the Prince of Peace."

When the pastor finished reading, he closed his Bible, bowed his head, and softly said, "His name is Wonderful." At that moment, something happened to Audrey Mieir that she had never experienced before. She heard a rustling sound, like the movement of wings. Then words came to her, words that she scribbled in the flyleaf of her Bible as fast as she could write them:

> His name is Wonderful,
> His name is Wonderful,
> His name is Wonderful,
> Jesus, my Lord.

Then another verse came to her, just like that:

> He is the Mighty King,
> Master of everything,
> His name is Wonderful,
> Jesus, my Lord.

Audrey had written other songs before, but none had ever come to her like that. She put the words to music that afternoon and taught it to the young people of the church that night. Later, over a burger and a soda, she composed the rest of the song, "His Name Is Wonderful." Little did Audrey know what impact those words would have in future years. This song had made its way into churches around the world, and has been translated into every major dialect. On one occasion it was sung simultaneously in four languages at the Vatican in the presence of the pope. And it all began with that verse of scripture from Isaiah 9.[3]

When Isaiah wrote that verse in the 8th century BC, little did he know what impact his words would have in future years. Isaiah thought he was writing about his present situation, a dark and fearsome time for the Jewish people. Tiglath-Pileser, the mighty warrior king of Assyria, had conquered the northern kingdom of Israel, and now the regions of Judah also were threatened. In the midst of this national crisis, Isaiah foretold of a king in the line of David who would deliver the people from destruction and usher in an everlasting era of peace.

In that time, it was customary for a new king to be given a series of exalted titles. The King James Version put a comma between the first two words, Wonderful and Counselor, as if they were two different titles. Most modern translations treat the two words as belonging together, so that Wonderful Counselor is the first of four titles ascribed to the new king. The other three titles are Mighty God (or Divine Warrior), Eternal Father, and Prince of Peace. Scholars speculate that Isaiah was referring to King Hezekiah, or perhaps King Josiah, as the promised child. But of course, neither Hezekiah nor Josiah fulfilled this messianic prophecy.

In 1741, George Frederic Handel was at one of the lowest points in his life. His health was failing, his popularity as a composer was waning, his audiences were deserting him, and he was deeply in debt. His life and work seemed to have little meaning or future. But then two opportunities came before him almost simultaneously that would change his life forever: A Dublin charity commissioned Handel to compose a piece of music for a benefit concert. And Charles Jennings, a wealthy friend, sent him a libretto based entirely on texts from the Bible. With libretto in hand, Handel went to work.

For three weeks, from early morning until late into the night, Handel hunched over his music paper, pens, and ink. A visitor during this time reported Handel weeping with intense emotion. At another point a servant went into Handel's room with a tray of food, but the weeping Handel refused to eat. In the incredibly short span of 24 days, Handel's oratorio, *Messiah*, was finished, including orchestration. Many musicologists consider it the greatest feat in the history of music composition.

In the midst of great depression, God inspired Handel to set this prophecy of Isaiah to majestic music. Who could forget that magnificent chorus, with the powerful refrain, "And his name shall be call-ed, Wonderful!" *Messiah* makes it plain that the prophecy of Isaiah was fulfilled in Jesus. Indeed, because of that chorus from the oratorio, I doubt that any Christian could read this prophecy and not think of Jesus. When we hear the words, "unto us a child is born, unto us a son is given," we automatically think about Jesus. And the titles make us think about Jesus too: "Wonderful Counselor, Mighty God, Everlasting Father, Prince of Peace." To be sure, Jesus was not the kind of king Isaiah was expecting. Jesus never had political power, nor ran a government, nor ruled a country. But while political kings and secular rulers have come and gone, Jesus remains the king of human hearts.

In 1996 my family was in Louisville, Kentucky for the funeral of my wife's mother. While we were there, I noticed an unusual ad in the September 21 issue of the *Louisville Courier-Journal* with a cryptic message that simply read: "I LOVE YOU EMILY." I came to find out that the same ad had been running every day since early in the year. Columnist Bob Hill also had seen the ad, and it piqued his curiosity. He contacted workers in the classified ad department to see if they could tell him anything, but citing confidentiality rules, they refused. Then he ran a notice in one of his columns, asking his readers if anyone knew anything about the ad.

A woman, who had a daughter named Emily, replied. The mother explained that her daughter, a fine athlete and aspiring ballet dancer, had been a psychology major at the University of Louisville. But in May of 1995, Emily was involved in a terrible automobile accident. She was a passenger in a car that was struck by another car making an illegal turn. Emily suffered severe, multiple injuries. Her liver was almost severed. Her spinal cord was injured, her wrist was crushed, and she had five broken ribs and a collapsed lung. The night after the accident she spent more than six hours in surgery. She was alive, but barely. Over the next two months in the hospital, Emily was given 11 units of blood. Several times she had heart irregularities and her liver malfunctioned. More than once Emily nearly died.

Emily's boyfriend, Tony, stood by her through it all. Eventually, she was discharged from the hospital to slowly recuperate at home. On the anniversary of the accident, Tony took out an ad in the newspaper that read, "I LOVE YOU EMILY." Tony ordered the ad only once, but it began to run every day.

The columnist reported that eventually Emily was able to return to school. Her back still hurt, her wrist still gave her problems, but she was getting on with her life. She was a little embarrassed by all the attention, but the ad was still running. No one knew who was paying for it. Emily and her family didn't know if it were a neighbor or a relative or a former boyfriend or some unconnected anonymous benefactor. All they knew is that when they saw the ad, they felt grateful—grateful that Emily was still alive, and grateful that someone cared.

When God sent Jesus, it was like he was taking out a classified ad to the world, saying, "I LOVE YOU." And day after day, that reminder is still here, making us grateful to be alive, grateful that someone cares. Yes, "his name is Wonderful, his name is Wonderful, his name is Wonderful, Jesus our Lord."

QUESTIONS FOR DISCUSSION/REFLECTION

1. Can you think of a time when you were walking in darkness?
2. In what sense has the Light dawned on you?
3. What does it mean for you that "a child is born to us"?
4. Which of the four titles—Wonderful Counselor, Mighty God, Eternal Father, Prince of Peace—has meaning for you? Why?
5. What hope does this prophecy from so long ago give to you today?

NOTES

[1] From a sermon by Peter J. Flamming, in his book, *Poking Holes in the Darkness* (Monument Avenue Press, 1992).

[2] Quoted in *Newsweek*, Dec. 1, 1986.

[3] From an article in *Worship Leader*, November/December, 1996.

CHAPTER 2

THE BIRTH OF JESUS CHRIST
(Matt. 1:18-25)

"Joseph son of David, don't be afraid to take Mary as your wife, because the child she carries was conceived by the Holy Spirit. She will give birth to a son, and you will call him Jesus, because he will save his people from their sins."

(Matt. 1:20b-21 CEB)

In the Bible, dreams sometimes convey a message from God. Joseph had a dream, and it changed his life! He was engaged to Mary, but when he learned that Mary was pregnant, he decided to call off the wedding to save face and to minimize the disgrace Mary might have experienced. We are not told how Mary became pregnant by the Holy Spirit (Luke fills in a lot of details in his gospel). But a pregnant unmarried woman was scandalous, nonetheless. An angel appeared to Joseph in a dream and told him not to be afraid to marry Mary. Her pregnancy was not due to unfaithfulness on her part, but faithfulness from God. The child she would bear was conceived by the Holy Spirit, as the fulfillment of Isaiah's prophecy from long ago (Isa. 7:14). Joseph, in the lineage of David, was instructed to name him Jesus, which means "Savior." Isaiah had called him Emmanuel, which means "God with us." Either way, God is with us to save us from our sins.

EMMANUEL
(Isa. 7:14, Matt. 1:18-23)

The year was 734 BC and King Ahaz of Judah was in a heap of trouble. His two neighbors to the north, the kingdoms of Syria and Israel, were poised to attack Judah unless he agreed to join their military coalition against the Assyrians. Ahaz was so frightened by their armies that he and his advisors shook like trees in the wind. Despite his fear of Syria and Israel, Ahaz feared Assyria even more. He did not think that the three smaller nations had a chance to defeat the powerful Assyrian army. So, his political instincts told him that the prudent move would be to align Judah with the enemy Ahaz. He entered into a pact with the Assyrians, even if it meant war with his neighbors. It was a calculated political gamble, but Ahaz saw no other option.

Isaiah did not like this move and told Ahaz it was a mistake to place his trust in political alliances. Instead, Isaiah said, Ahaz should trust in God. And in good prophetic tradition, Isaiah said that God would give Ahaz a sign: A young woman would have a baby, a son, and she would name him Immanuel, which means, "God is with us."

To be honest, we don't know if that prophecy was fulfilled in Isaiah's lifetime. We have no record of a child being named Immanuel. But almost eight centuries later, Matthew remembered the prophecy when he wrote about the birth of Jesus. Matthew and the early Christians believed that Jesus was the fulfillment of the ancient prophecy.

Of course, the political situation was vastly different in Matthew's time. When Jesus was born, the Assyrians were long gone from the world scene as a military threat. The Romans were the mighty power then. But Matthew did not understand the prophecy to refer to a military leader. He interpreted it to refer to the coming of a child who would represent the very presence of God.

We don't know that Jesus was ever called Emmanuel, except in Matthew's gospel. The name Immanuel is mentioned only three times in the Bible—twice in Isaiah and once in Matthew. In Isaiah, Immanuel is spelled with an "I." In Matthew, Emmanuel is spelled with an "E." That is why we see it in English with both spellings. But whether we spell it with an "I" or with an "E," the message is the same: The birth of a child is a sign that God is with us. The name Emmanuel is a symbol of God's guiding, protecting presence with his people.

Isaiah encouraged King Ahaz to trust in God in a time of national crisis. Instead, Ahaz trusted in his own political instincts, and eventually Judah became a vassal state of the Assyrian empire. But looking back eight centuries later, Matthew recognized that the prophecy had nothing to do with political alliances. Rather, the prophecy had to do with God becoming involved in the affairs of humankind. And as Matthew sought to explain the meaning of the birth of Jesus, he saw that the name Emmanuel was a perfect description of who Jesus was and what Jesus came to do. Jesus was "God with us," and Jesus came to represent God's presence in our lives.

We need the promise of Emmanuel because we live in a time of crisis, too. The threats we fear are not necessarily from an invading army. Although the threat of terrorism is real, and foreign espionage is still a problem, and nuclear proliferation jeopardizes our security, our more imminent threats are internal—threats from a society that seems to be pulling apart. Incivility is on the rise. Recalcitrant racism, drug use, alcohol addiction, child abuse, a burgeoning prison population, and a global pandemic: Almost everywhere you turn there is bad news. The crisis in our time is a world spinning out of control without God. As Yeats said in his poem, "turning and turning in the widening gyre, the falcon cannot hear the falconer."

We live in a world that has largely lost any sense of God's presence. There is a breakdown of morality, the absence of a moral compass. And there are also personal crises that threaten our well-being. Whether it is a health crisis, or financial worries, or marriage or family crises, or other concerns, they intrude upon us as unwelcome guests. That is why we need the message of Emmanuel. God is here. We are not alone. We are not without hope. God has invaded our history and our hearts with love.

One of my favorite works of art, and one of the most famous paintings in the world, is Michelangelo's fresco on the ceiling of the Sistine Chapel in Rome. In that huge mural depicting the story of Creation, one can see the muscular arm of God extending his index finger down to the figure of Adam, whose finger is stretched out toward heaven. The two fingers do not touch, but we can envision the spark of life flowing from the hand of God to man. In a magazine ad, an investment company reproduced the famous painting in vivid color. Underneath the picture was the caption, "Sometimes success is a matter of making the right connection." That is the message of Christmas. The success of our lives is a matter of making the right connection. And while we could never reach to heaven, God has reached down to us through the person of his Son and touched us with his life-giving love.

The contemporary Christian poet-singer-songwriter Michael Card put it like this in the first few verses of his song, "Immanuel":

A sign shall be given
A virgin will conceive
A human baby bearing
Undiminished deity
The glory of the nations
A light for all to see
That hope for all who will embrace
His warm reality

Immanuel
Our God is with us
And if God is with us
Who could stand against us
Our God is with us

Immanuel.
For all those who live in the shadow of death
A glorious light has dawned
For all those who stumble in the darkness
Behold your light has come

JOSEPH: PEACE
(Matt. 1:18-25)

Everyone dreams. I'm not talking about daydreaming, although most people do that. Nor am I talking about planning for the future, although most of us do that too. I'm talking about what happens when we sleep at night. We dream. It usually happens during a type of sleep known as REM (Rapid Eye Movement), when our eyes move rapidly beneath our closed eyelids. These REM sleep episodes can last anywhere from 5-20 minutes in duration, and they occur periodically throughout the night. A typical person spends about two hours every night dreaming, which may seem like a lot, but that is because we don't remember most of our dreams. In fact, we forget about 95 percent of them. The best chance of remembering a dream is if we wake up during REM sleep, especially if it is the last dream of the night and we wake up while the dream is still going on.

The content of our dreams can range from routine and ordinary to bizarre and surreal. Most of my dreams—at least the ones I remember—are somewhere between boring and weird. My dreams typically include places and people I know, but there are often strange circumstances or unexpected twists that make the dreams hard to understand. Many people believe that their dreams have some meaning. Sigmund Freud called dreams "the royal road to the unconscious." Carl Jung believed that dreams were messages that could help the dreamer resolve emotional issues or problems. Jung believed that memories from each day would leave impressions for the unconscious to deal with them. Jung called these impressions "day residue."

The most common emotion that people say they experience when they dream is anxiety, which makes sense if dreams usually deal with unresolved issues. People also report experiencing fear, anger, abandonment, and happiness in their dreams. Negative emotions during dreams seem to occur more frequently than positive feelings. Maybe it is a good thing that we forget the majority of our dreams.

Dreams in the Bible were often seen as having some spiritual meaning. That is not surprising because during the Greek and Roman eras, dreams were viewed as messages from the gods, or messages from the dead. Sometimes dreams were seen as forewarnings or predictions about the future. Sometimes people looked to dreams to tell them what action to take in a difficult situation. For Jews and Christians in biblical times, dreams were often interpreted as messages from God.

In our scripture passage Joseph had a dream. Joseph, you recall, was a carpenter from Nazareth who was engaged to be married to a virgin named Mary. They were not yet living together as husband and wife, and they certainly would have no marital relations until after they were married. So, when Joseph found out that his fiancée was pregnant, he faced a difficult moral dilemma. Joseph cared for Mary, but there was no way he could go ahead with the wedding if she were pregnant, especially since he knew the child could not be his. So, Joseph resolved to dismiss her quietly, to cancel the engagement and call off the wedding with as little fanfare as possible, to try to minimize her public disgrace and his own humiliation. Still, Joseph had trouble finding peace in this "necessary" decision. On the one hand, he was a righteous man who sought to do what was moral. On the other hand, cultural standards of morality do not always square with doing what feels right. Because he really cared about Mary, Joseph struggled with dismissing her, even if he did it quietly. It just did not feel right.

While Joseph was in the midst of this difficult moral dilemma, he may have begun to second-guess his decision to break off the engagement and call off the wedding. His head told him it was the right thing to do, but his heart said otherwise. His heart could not believe that Mary had been unfaithful to him, although intellectually how else could he explain her unplanned pregnancy? My guess is that while Joseph was wrestling in his own mind with what was the right thing to do, he had this dream. An angel of the Lord appeared to Joseph in the dream and said, "Joseph, son of David, do not be afraid to take Mary as your wife, for the child conceived in her is from the Holy Spirit." Like I said, many dreams are a mixture of the ordinary and the bizarre. Who ever heard of a child conceived by the Holy Spirit? No way Joseph could have made this up! But there was more. Not only was this child conceived by the Holy Spirit, but this child also would save people from their sins. That was why Joseph was instructed by the angel to name the child Jesus, which in the Hebrew *Yeshua* means "God will save."

Maybe Carl Jung was right when he said that some dreams help us to find solutions to unresolved issues. This dream helped Joseph resolve the issue of what he should do about Mary. Joseph remembered this dream, and it inspired him to change his mind and change his plans. In fact, Joseph came to realize that Mary's pregnancy was the fulfillment of an ancient prophecy from Isaiah. When Joseph awoke from his dream, he did what the angel said. He took Mary as his wife, even though their marriage would subject both of them to scandal. The two lived together as husband and wife, but they had no marital relations until after Mary gave birth to her son. Joseph named the child Jesus.

It is not always easy to know what is the right thing to do. Life sometimes finds us at cross purposes when we are pulled in different directions by competing loyalties. That which is legal and that which is right are not always the same thing. Joseph could have called out Mary, and no one would have blamed him for exposing her to public disgrace. Joseph could have accused Mary of infidelity and demanded that she be stoned to death. That was the legal thing to do, but Joseph did not feel good about it. He resolved to dismiss her quietly, but he did not feel good about that either. So, he struggled with doing the right thing. As he wrestled with that unresolved issue, Joseph had a dream. And in that dream an angel of the Lord helped Joseph figure out the right thing to do.

I think the reason Joseph struggled with doing the right thing is that even before he had the dream, he valued Mary as a person. He did not want any harm to come to her. He did not want her to be exposed to public disgrace. He certainly did not want her to be stoned to death. In fact, Joseph wanted to protect and defend Mary, even before he understood the circumstances of her pregnancy. Joseph struggled with doing the right thing because he understood that people are more important than worrying about what others might say. In the end, Joseph was more concerned about Mary than about his own reputation. He had a dream, and because of that dream, Joseph changed his mind and changed his plans. Instead of dismissing Mary, Joseph took her as his wife. No doubt, there were plenty of stares and gossip and ridicule, but Joseph did not care. He finally had peace—peace in his mind, peace in his heart—because he had done the right thing.

Sometimes life presents us with difficult decisions that keep us awake at night or that torment us in our dreams. But if we will listen for the voice of God, even in our sleep, we will find the peace that only comes from doing the right thing. And then it does not matter what anyone else says. The author Isaac Asimov wrote, "Never let your sense of morals prevent you from doing what's right." So, Joseph took Mary as his wife, and when her child was born, Joseph named him Jesus. And Jesus did save people from their sins. Jesus did the right thing, and through his sacrifice, he gave us peace with God.

GOD WITH US
(Matt. 1:18-25)

It's the same quandary every year—what to give people for Christmas. The problem is, most of the people on my Christmas list already have everything they need. Still, I want to give them something as a token of my friendship or love. So, I seek something that will be appropriate, something that will be appreciated, something that will reflect how I feel about them. It is a yearly ordeal for me—Christmas shopping—because I continually struggle to find just the right gift for the people I care about.

God did not have that problem that first Christmas. God knew exactly what people on his list really need, and God gave us the perfect gift. For Joseph, however, God's perfect gift was more of a dilemma than a delight. When Joseph found out that Mary was with child, it did not seem like a gift at all. Joseph and Mary were engaged to be married. They were officially betrothed. Betrothal was a legally binding agreement. While the couple did not yet live together, they were expected to be faithful to one another. A young woman whose fiancé died during this period of betrothal was called "a virgin who is a widow." The only way to undo a betrothal was to go through a formal divorce. Usually, this time of betrothal lasted a year. Then the woman would leave her parents' home and go to live with her husband. At that point, the marriage would be consummated, and they would live together in a monogamous union of fidelity and trust.

Imagine Joseph's shock, embarrassment, and outrage when he discovered that Mary was pregnant. The child could not be his since they had not yet come together. Joseph could only conclude that Mary had betrayed his trust and been unfaithful to him. Joseph had two options: He could charge Mary publicly with adultery and have her arrested and brought to trial. Or, he could divorce her quietly and try to limit her shame—and his own.

Adultery was a serious offense, punishable by death. Joseph did not want to see Mary hurt, so he resolved to take the kinder course and call off the wedding, with as little fanfare as possible. He would break the engagement privately, without pressing charges. It was then that Joseph had a dream. An angel appeared in his sleep and explained that Mary had not been unfaithful after all. The baby she would bear was a gift of God's Spirit. The baby was a gift to Mary, and a gift to Joseph too. The angel told Joseph to take Mary as his bride, and to name the baby after it was born. When a father named a child, he assumed responsibility for that child, acknowledging the child as his own. The name for the baby would be Jesus. In Greek, the name was *Jesu*; in Hebrew, the name was *Jeshua*, which means "Yahweh is salvation." Not only did this baby have a special origin; this baby had a special mission. This baby would save people from their sins.

Martin Luther said, "the greatest miracle of Christmas was not that Mary conceived but that Joseph believed." The poet W.H. Auden called Joseph "the first Christian," because Joseph believed even though he did not fully understand. It took a leap of faith for Joseph to risk public ridicule and go ahead with the wedding. But he sensed that there was something more here than the scandal of an illegitimate birth. Joseph sensed that God was in it. And so, in that respect, Joseph was the first Christian. He believed that God was active in his own life, and he acted on that belief.

Isn't it remarkable how God often chooses to work in what would otherwise be negative circumstances? God must have a wonderful sense of humor, because he often chooses the least likely situations and the least likely persons to accomplish his purposes. The Son of God conceived out of wedlock? Born to a carpenter and a peasant girl? Sheltered in a stable? Cradled in a manger? Visited by shepherds, the lowest class of people? Visited next, not by the respectable leaders of Israel, but by Gentile astrologers? The whole story is filled with unexpected surprises. Maybe that is the way God operates—with surprises. Maybe it is in the toughest situations of life that God is most likely to be found.

Gerald Coffee was a captain in the United States Navy during the Vietnam War. His plane was shot down over North Vietnam, and he was captured and held as a prisoner of war. His third Christmas in captivity was in 1968. He remembered it because his Vietnamese prison guards gave him three candy bars for Christmas that year. The candy bars were wrapped in foil with red on the outside and silver on the inside. Captain Coffee was held in solitary confinement in a cell with a dirt floor and a bare yellow light bulb hanging from the ceiling. His only furnishings were a bed of straw mats and a crude broom fashioned from a bundle of straws. The candy bars were the only things that made Christmas different from any other day.

Captain Coffee flattened one of the candy bar wrappers and folded it into the shape of an origami swan. He took the second wrapper, flattened it, and folded it into a rosette, using a piece of thread to tie the pleats in the center while he fanned out the edges. With the third wrapper, he fashioned a star. He removed three straws from his broom and stuck them into cracks in the wall above his bed. Then he hung the three candy wrapper ornaments on the straws over his bed. Lying down on the mat, he looked up at the ornaments and celebrated Christmas. This is how he described the experience:

> Here there was nothing to distract me from the awesomeness of Christmas—no commercialism, no presents, little food. I was beginning to appreciate my own spirituality, because I had been stripped of everything by which I had measured my identity—rank, uniform, money, family. Yet, I continued to find strength within. I realized that although I was hurting and lonely and scared, this might be the most significant Christmas of my life.[1]

Imagine, the most significant Christmas of his life—alone in a tiny room halfway around the world, with candy wrapper ornaments dangling from straws stuck in cracks in the wall. Somehow God does come in the most unlikely of places—a prison cell in North Vietnam or a stable in Bethlehem. Somehow God comes at the most unlikely times and unlikely circumstances of our lives. Somehow God comes when the nights are cold and dark, and the days are long and lonely. Somehow God comes.

A little girl proudly presented her mother with a finger painting she had made in Sunday School. Across the top of the picture the teacher had written, "Jesus and the children." The mother looked at the painting. It was filled with faces, round happy faces, all just the same. She started to ask her daughter which one was Jesus, but then she realized it did not matter. Jesus was there someplace among the children, and that was all that mattered.

That is the message of Christmas. God is with us. God is here in the unlikely places and unlikely times of our lives. God is with us, and that is all that matters. God has come to love us and to save us. God saves us by loving us. That is the promise of Christmas.

God does not promise a long nor carefree life. God does not promise prosperity or success or good health. God only promises to be with us and to never leave us. And somehow that is enough.

What do you want for Christmas? What do you really need? God has the perfect gift for you—one that God made himself. It is a gift that is the very essence of love. Like Joseph, you don't have to understand everything about God's gift. All you have to do is believe it and accept it. Then, like Joseph, your life will never be the same.

> That was no time for a child to be born,
> In a land in the crushing grip of Rome;
> Honour and truth were trampled by score—
> Yet here did the Saviour make his home.
>
> When is the time for love to be born?
> The inn is full on the planet earth.
> And by a comet the sky is torn—
> Yet Love still takes the risk of birth.
> Yet Love still takes the risk of birth.
>
> —*Madeleine L'Engle*[2]

QUESTIONS FOR DISCUSSION/REFLECTION

1. What is the meaning of Jesus being conceived by the Holy Spirit?
2. In what ways was Joseph a righteous man?
3. Has God ever spoken to you in a dream or in another way?
4. In what ways was Jesus the fulfillment of prophecy?
5. What is the meaning of the name "Jesus" for you?

NOTES

[1] Told by Gerald Coffee in *Readers Digest*, December 1989.
[2] "The Risk of Birth, An Advent Poem," 1973.

CHAPTER 3

VISIT OF THE WISE MEN
(Matt. 2:1-12)

When they saw the star, they were filled with joy. They entered the house and saw the child with Mary his mother. Falling to their knees, they honored him. Then they … presented him with gifts of gold, frankincense, and myrrh.

(Matt. 2:10-11 CEB)

Not only is the visit of the wise men to the infant Jesus a good story, but it is also the basis for Epiphany Sunday in many churches every year in January. Thus, it is one of the best known and most beloved stories in the Bible. The wise men, or magi, are sometimes called kings—hence the beginning of the Christmas carol, "We three kings of Orient are; bearing gifts we traverse afar." The assumption that there were three of them is based on the three gifts they brought to pay homage to the newly born king. Although Matthew recounts this story immediately after he tells about the birth of Jesus, the visit of the magi may have occurred some months later. Mary and Joseph were living in a house in Bethlehem with the child Jesus when the wise men arrived. Since they were no longer in the stable where Jesus had been born and laid in the manger (according to Luke's gospel), we assume that the family had taken up residence in Bethlehem, at least for a while.

Magi were stargazers, presumably from Persia, who assigned earthly events to heavenly signs. Today we might call them astrologers. They made the connection between a new star and a newborn king of the Jews. Naturally, they came to Jerusalem expecting to find the new king there. Herod, the incumbent king of the Jews, was none too pleased to learn of a possible rival to his throne. Consulting with scholars of the Hebrew scriptures, he learned that the prophet Micah had predicted that Bethlehem would produce a shepherd king like David to rule the people of Israel (Mic. 5:2). In the chance that the prophecy might somehow be fulfilled, Herod sent the wise men to Bethlehem to search diligently for the child. We learn from the second part of the story (Matt. 2:13-23) that Herod's intent was not to honor the child but to kill him. Being warned in a dream not to return to King Herod, the wise men returned home by another way.

GIFTS FOR A KING
(Matt. 2:1-12)

One of my favorite columnists for *The Washington Post* is Michelle Singletary, who writes a financial column called "The Color of Money." I like Michelle not only because she offers practical advice about money, but also because she writes from a Christian perspective. She is an active member of a local Baptist church in suburban Maryland, and she even conducts financial seminars in her church. In a column she wrote for the newspaper, she asked the question, "Do your finances reflect your values?"

Every year since 2001, the Gallup organization has polled Americans about their finances. In 2016, Gallup found that Americans' greatest financial concerns were about retirement, being able to cover a major healthcare crisis, and sustaining a suitable standard of living. But those are not the only financial concerns people have. Many people are concerned about having enough money to pay their monthly bills or to make minimum credit card payments. Money is an important subject for most people.

Michelle Singletary pushed the question even further by asking, "Are you spending your money in the areas you truly value?" She quoted one of her favorite scripture verses, from Jesus in the Sermon on the Mount: "For where you treasure is, there your heart will be also" (Matt. 6:21). Michelle said if you want to find out what you truly value, if you want to measure your heart's desires, just look at your bank or credit card statements to see where your money goes. Where your treasure is, there will your heart be also. What we truly value is revealed by how we spend our money.

Our scripture passage is one of the most familiar stories surrounding the birth of Jesus. The visit of the wise men is so well known that there is even a day on the Christian calendar devoted to it—Epiphany. Every year we celebrate Epiphany Sunday, commemorating the coming of the magi to pay homage to the newborn king of the Jews. The magi, or wise men, were not Jews. They were Gentiles, probably from Persia, or modern-day Iran. They seem to have been astrologers since they studied the stars to discern the meaning of events on earth. The wise men noticed a new star they had never seen before, and concluded that it announced the birth of a new king of the Jews.

The wise men made the long journey from their homeland to Jerusalem, since they assumed that a new king of the Jews would be born there. Needless to say, the current ruler of the Jews, King Herod, was not happy about a possible rival to his throne. But Herod played along with the wise men to gain their trust and to ascertain where a new king of the Jews might be born. On the basis of a prophecy in the Jewish scriptures, Herod's own "wise men" determined that Bethlehem was the place the Messiah, the anointed one, would be born.

So, Herod sent the Gentile wise men to Bethlehem, with the instruction that if they should find the new king, they would return to Herod. The purpose was to give him a report, so that he too might go and worship the new king. Of course, we know that Herod's intent was not so benevolent. Herod's intent was not to worship the new king, but to destroy him. But as the wise men left Jerusalem for Bethlehem, they were overjoyed to see that the star they had followed appeared again. The star led them, not to the manger, but to a house where Jesus was living. On entering the house, the wise men found the child with Mary his mother. They knelt to pay him homage. Then, opening their treasure chests, they offered him gifts of gold, frankincense, and myrrh.

This story is so familiar that we might easily miss its meaning. We know about the three gifts. In fact, because they offered three gifts, we assume that there were three wise men, even though they are not specified as three. Of the three gifts, gold is the most recognizable. Gold was, and is, valuable. Last I checked, gold was selling for more than $1,900 an ounce! Frankincense and myrrh were also valuable. The first-century Roman scholar Pliny wrote that a pound of frankincense cost six denarii, equal to six days wages of a day laborer. In today's terms, at minimum wage, that would equal more than $500 for a pound of frankincense. Pliny wrote that myrrh went for 50 denarii a pound, or roughly $4400. Matthew does not say how much gold, frankincense, and myrrh the wise men gave Jesus, whether an ounce, or a pound, or more. But at that time, these were three of the most valuable commodities anyone might carry in their treasure chests. They were gifts fit for a king, probably worth thousands of dollars. If you traveled hundreds of miles to pay homage to a king, you would not offer the king cheap junk; you would present the king with the best you have. The wise men showed how much they valued Jesus by offering him their best. Do we do the same?

What we give to God is vitally important. Many people already know how important charitable giving is. But maybe Michelle Singletary has a point. Maybe we do need to re-evaluate, from time to time, how we spend our money. Maybe we need to make sure that our spending accurately reflects our values. Epiphany, near the beginning of a new year, is a good time to make such an assessment. It may be that our spending has lost its focus. It may be that we are devoting too much of our money to things of lesser value, and not devoting enough of our money to what we truly value.

What are your greatest values? Or, to put it another way, what are your treasures? For me, my greatest values, my treasures, are God, my family, my health, my friends, and my church. I also value my home, my retirement and savings accounts, my pastoral library, my golf clubs, my clothing, and other material things. And I value nonmaterial things, too. I value spending time with my wife Linda, especially when we can get away on vacation. I value my country. I value freedom. I value the opportunity to help others. The question is: Do I spend my money according to my values?

The wise men offered gifts of great value to Jesus because Jesus was of value to them. Jesus is of value to us. What gifts do we offer to reflect our love and devotion to him?

Linda and I decided at the beginning of our marriage to tithe a tenth of our income to the Lord's work. In those early years of our life together, our income was not very much. My combined salary and housing allowance in my first job after seminary totaled $12,000 a year. We had a hard time getting by on $12,000 a year, so the church increased it to $13,000 the next year. But even when I was not making very much, we felt it was important to tithe a tenth of our income to the Lord's work. And we have continued to tithe every year since then. Add in special offerings, and we typically give more than a tenth of our income to the church.

Linda and I give to the church for three reasons. First, the church needs our gifts. Because most churches do not have an endowment fund or outside source of income, they could not exist without the tithes and freewill offerings of the people in the congregation. What people put into the offering plates or donate online fund the ministries of the church. The only way most churches can stay in business is through the tithes and offerings of the people.

Second, we give because we need to give. Generosity is good for our spiritual condition. Generous people are happier, more fulfilled, and more satisfied. When I give, I feel better about myself because I am using my money to make a positive difference in the world. Being generous helps me to be less selfish and self-centered. Generosity is good for the soul.

Third, we give because God deserves our gratitude for all he has given to us. The Bible tells us that "God is love" and that "God's love was revealed among us in this way: God sent his only Son into the world so that we might live through him" (1 John 4:8-9).

The wise men gave Jesus precious gifts of gold, frankincense, and myrrh. We give Jesus precious gifts of money—either by cash or check or online. The point is not how we give, but that we give. Giving is an act of worship. It is one way we show God how much we love him. Paul wrote: "Each of you must give as you have made up your mind, not reluctantly or under compulsion, for God loves a cheerful giver" (2 Cor. 9:7).

If Jesus were here right now, what would you give him? Well, he is here. He is with us always. May we give, not reluctantly, but cheerfully, generously, joyfully.

TAKE ME TO THE KING
(Matt. 2:1-12)

After our granddaughter Ford was born in 2015, Linda and I made a trip from Maryland to California to see her. Ford was only five weeks old. We spent most of the time just looking at her, holding her, playing with her, talking to her, and otherwise being enchanted by her. Something about a baby inspires people to travel a long distance just to pay a visit.

The wise men traveled a long distance to visit the baby Jesus. At first, they did not know his name. All they knew is that a baby had been born, a child they identified as the king of the Jews. The wise men were not Jews. They were from the East, probably from Persia, the region we know today as Iran. Apparently, they were stargazers, a cross between astronomers and astrologers. Back then, wise men would study the heavens for celestial signs. They had seen a star at its rising and interpreted this phenomenon to be a sign of a newborn king of the Jews. They had traveled to Jerusalem, where they naturally expected the king of the Jews to be born, to pay him homage.

Such a long journey was not as improbable as it might sound. At that time wise men saw connections between astral signs and political events, especially the rise and fall of kings. They believed something new in the heavens signaled something new on earth. A long journey to visit a king was not as unusual as it might appear. For example, ancient historians Cassius Dio and Suetonius chronicled the visit of a Persian wise man named Tiridates to the Emperor Nero in Rome in AD 66. Traveling from Persia to Jerusalem would not have been nearly as long a distance as traveling from Persia to Rome. So, it was not inconceivable that wise men would have made such a journey to Jerusalem in search of a newborn king. With the belief that stars could herald the birth of a human destined for greatness, the wise men came to Herod's palace asking, "Where is the child who has been born king of the Jews?" Again, secular historians confirm the plausibility of such an occurrence. Suetonius and Tacitus both wrote that at that time there was great expectation of a world ruler coming from Judea.

When Herod heard about the journey of the wise men, and the newborn king of the Jews they were seeking, he was frightened. Herod was the king of the Jews, and the possibility of a new king threatened him. The irony is that Herod was not Jewish. He had become king of the Jews through military conquest and political alliance with Rome. Herod's ethnic background was Idumean, meaning he was of Edomite heritage. He had become king of the Jews because Rome wanted him to be the king of the Jews.

In many respects, Herod was an odd choice, because he did not follow all the teachings of the Jewish religion. For example, he had no hesitation worshipping the Roman emperor or supporting temple cults such as Pythian Apollo. Herod did rebuild the Temple in Jerusalem, but it was one of his many building projects as a tribute to himself. So long as Herod was willing to do Rome's bidding and levy exorbitant taxes on the Jewish people, Rome was willing to put up with Herod's megalomania.

The older Herod got, the more paranoid he became. Sometime around 7 BC, shortly before Jesus was born, Herod had two of his own sons executed on charges of treason. Later, he had yet another son by another wife executed. During the last two years of his life Herod drew up three different wills, each time changing whom he had chosen to succeed him upon his death. Herod had such a bloodthirsty reputation that the Roman emperor, Caesar Augustus, used a play on words. Augustus joked that it was better to be Herod's pig (*hus*) than Herod's son (*huios*). Given Herod's fear of rivals to his throne, it is easy to understand that the question from the wise men would have troubled him: "Where is the child that has been born king of the Jews?"

Summoning his own wise men, Herod learned from them where the Messiah was to be born: "In Bethlehem of Judea; for so it has been written by the prophet." Herod secretly summoned the wise men, ascertaining from them what time the star had appeared. Then he sent them on to Bethlehem, six miles away, saying, "Search diligently for the child, and when you have found him, bring me word so that I may go and pay him homage." Of course, Herod's true intent was not benevolent at all.

The wise men set out, and they followed the star to Bethlehem, to the place where the child was. Not everything in the story is easy to explain, such as the guiding star that stopped over the place where the child was. Typically, stars do not move and then stop over a specific location. Johannes Kepler, the 16th-century German mathematician-astronomer-astrologer, recognized that this star was not a typical astral phenomenon. Kepler conjectured that the star was the birth of a super nova, which stargazers might well have interpreted to signal the birth of a new king.

The wise men were overwhelmed with joy as they entered the house and saw the child with his mother Mary. Note that the family was now staying in a house, not a stable. The wise men knelt and paid homage. It was an act of respect, honor, and worship. Opening their treasure chests, they gave him gifts of gold, frankincense, and myrrh. Finally, being warned in a dream not to return to Herod, the wise men returned home by another way. Eventually Herod would learn that he had been tricked by the wise men—but that is another story.

In this story we have Matthew's version of the birth of Jesus. Matthew does not tell us about the manger or the shepherds or the angels that appeared on the night that Jesus was born. Instead, Matthew picks up the story after that, with the visit of the wise men. In a sense, the visit of the Gentile wise men foreshadows the Gentile world that would eventually come to Jesus, including most of us. It is as though Matthew wants us to recognize that the king of the Jews came not just for the Jews, but for all people. And it is as though Matthew wants us to understand that all of us are invited to come to Jesus with our worship and our gifts and our faith.

There is one more truth that the story of the wise men can teach us. When we meet Jesus, when we come to him with our worship and our gifts and our faith, that experience changes us. We are not the same; we go home another way. We live differently because Jesus is our king. We have different values, different priorities, a different outlook on life. Because Jesus is our king, we are citizens of another kingdom. We are in the world, but not of the world. We live in time, but we live for eternity. We go home another way.

Matthew does not tell us what happened to the wise men after they left Jesus to return to their own country. We know they did not go back to Herod, but what it meant for them to return by another way we can only imagine. If I were to guess, I would say they were changed men. A genuine encounter with Jesus changes us. It makes us new and better. It makes us kinder and more loving. It gives us a heart of compassion and a desire to live with integrity. Once you have met Jesus, once you acknowledge him as your king, then you cannot go back to only living for yourself. You recognize there is a greater purpose for your life, and you experience a joy the world cannot give.

The king of the Jews: that was what the wise men called him. The king of the Jews: that was the charge Pilate posted on his cross. Jesus would not have been crucified for being merely a rabbi or even a prophet; he was crucified for being a king. The wise men were right: he was the king of the Jews, and he would become the king of all who would believe in him. Yet, King Jesus rules not by might, but by love. "He humbled himself and became obedient to the point of death—even death on a cross. Therefore God also highly exalted him and gave him the name that is above every name, so that at the name of Jesus every knee should bend, in heaven and on earth and under the earth, and every tongue should confess that Jesus Christ is Lord, to the glory of God the Father" (Phil. 2:8-11).

There is a song by Tamela Mann that begins, "Take me to the king / I don't have much to bring / My heart is torn in pieces / It's my offering." All the king requires of us is a humble heart, a torn heart, a broken heart, an open heart, a heart ready to receive his love.

THE JOURNEY
(Matt. 2:1-12)

It is one of the best-known stories in the Bible, and perhaps among the least understood. Just about everything in the hymn "We Three Kings," is wrong. First, the visitors were not kings. The Greek word is *magi*, which means astrologers. Some versions of the Bible translate the word as "wise men," but these fellows were not kings. Second, we do not know how many of them came to see the newborn king of the Jews. They brought three kinds of gifts, but there could have been two, three, four, a dozen magi … who knows? Third, they were not from the Orient. The scripture says they were from the East. Most likely they were from Persia, which is modern-day Iran. Most of the nativity scenes get it wrong. The magi did not arrive in Bethlehem on the night Jesus was born. They did not gather around the manger with the shepherds. These were two separate events. The shepherds did come to the manger that night, but the magi arrived in Bethlehem later, where they found Mary and the child Jesus in a house. That is why we celebrate the visit of the magi on Epiphany Sunday, and not on Christmas Eve. This is a separate story.

Another thing we do not understand is why the magi made that journey at all. Yes, they were astrologers who studied the movement of the stars. Yes, they had observed a star "at its rising," which they interpreted to signal the birth of a new king. But why would they make such a journey? They were not Jews. Jesus was not their newborn king. What could possibly motivate those magi to leave their work, their families, and their country and undertake a costly and dangerous journey of hundreds of miles to pay homage to a baby they had no connection to at all? The whole story does not make a lot of sense, unless you read between the lines and try to imagine what would lead such magi to make such a journey in the first place.

Religious participation is waning in America. Oh, most people still say they believe in God, but fewer people are choosing to identify themselves with any religious organization. According to recent polls, many Americans now identify themselves as religiously unaffiliated. Some people say they are "spiritual but not religious." They have their own personal, private beliefs, but they choose not to join a church or attend religious services. Young adults in particular are becoming less and less religious.

According to the Pew Research Center, more than one-third of young adults under the age of 30 are religiously unaffiliated, the highest percentage ever recorded. There are many possible explanations for the decline in religious affiliation, especially among younger people. Our culture has become increasingly secular. Many businesses are now open on Sundays. For many people, watching football is more important than going to church. Religious participation is seldom depicted on television or in movies, except in a negative way. When was the last time you saw a positive portrayal in the media of people going to church? Our society is also becoming more disconnected. Membership in bowling leagues, hobby clubs, and alumni associations has been declining for years. People are increasingly reluctant to join any group or commit to any ongoing obligation.

The mixture of religion and politics has turned off a lot of people to religion. Harvard political scientist Robert Putnam believes that part of the decline in religious affiliation is a negative reaction to the Religious Right. Church teachings are perceived to be rigid and intolerant. In his book, *Bowling Alone*, Putnam wrote that Americans are fleeing religion and institutions in general.

Some people have reacted to religious extremism by rejecting religion altogether. One reader (Steve Agnew) responded to an online report about the decline in religious affiliation, writing this:

> Prior to 9-11, I viewed religion as an irrational but harmless part of most other people's lives. We can and do, after all, agree to live by the golden rule without the need for any divine story.
>
> After 9-11, my thinking changed dramatically. I came to realize that the irrational and ultimately destructive religio-political zealotry of radical Islam

was not unique among religious ideologies. Any of these religions also have the potential zealotry for persecution, war, inquisition, shunning, excommunication, and other religious punishments. Even Buddhism has its zealots.

Nevertheless, I now count myself as a believer, but I believe in science and metascience, not religion. Thank goodness that science will always explain the explainable. Although there are still some mysteries and gaps in scientific understanding, science nevertheless by definition explains the explainable.

But we also need spiritual or supernatural explanations for the inexplicable.[1]

I don't know anything about this writer, but I suspect he expresses the opinions of many people who have become disaffected by organized religion. Religious fanaticism and extremism are serious issues in our world today. People who claim to possess the ultimate truth and who are intolerant of other belief systems can cause great harm. But to dismiss all religious belief and practice because some religion has been corrupted by fanaticism is like banning all food because some people have become overweight from overeating. As the author admitted, "we need spiritual or supernatural explanations for the inexplicable." I too am a great believer in science, but science cannot explain everything. Science can explain how the world operates, but it cannot explain why.

I've been trying to come up with an explanation for why the magi made their journey to Bethlehem to find the newborn king of the Jews. The only reason I can come up with is that they were seekers of truth. They believed that the star in the sky would lead them to find it. We do not know much about the religion of the magi before they met Jesus, but we can assume they must have had some familiarity with the Hebrew Scriptures. How else could they have concluded that the star in the sky announced the birth of the king of the Jews? There was an ancient prophesy in the book of Numbers that "a star shall come out of Jacob, and a scepter shall rise out of Israel" (24:17). Perhaps the magi were familiar with that prophecy. Hence, they first came to Jerusalem looking for the newborn king of the Jews. Not finding him there, and being guided by another prophecy from the scriptures, they followed the star to the place where Jesus was. There they found the truth they had been seeking. Then, being warned in a dream not to return to Herod, they went home by another way.

Perhaps the journey of the magi is a parable of the journey of all those who seek the truth. Life itself is a journey, but only when we follow the scriptures and the signs that God provides will we come to know the truth. Maybe, like the magi, we need to lift our gaze above the things of earth to see the things of heaven. Maybe, like the magi, we need to believe that God still leads and directs our lives, if only we will have the faith to follow.

I was at home watching television, channel surfing, when I came across a program on Maryland Public Television called "direct connection." The moderator was interviewing a scientist from Goddard Space Flight Center who was involved with the Hubble Space Telescope program. I was amazed to learn that the Hubble has been orbiting the earth for some 30 years, peering further and further into the distant reaches of the universe. It has detected not only billions of stars, but also billions of galaxies. That is hard to imagine.

The earth is our world, but in terms of the total universe the earth is but a tiny speck of cosmic dust. Our solar system is just one of 200–400 billion stars that make up the Milky Way galaxy. And the Milky Way galaxy is just one of perhaps 100–200 billion galaxies in the universe. No one knows the exact number of galaxies because the Hubble and other telescopes have been able to deeply observe only a tiny fraction of the sky. But from what scientists have seen, they can estimate how many more galaxies they have yet to see. By studying the stars and other celestial phenomena, scientists are on their own journey to the truth.

The magi studied the heavens to seek the truth. And when they saw the "Bethlehem" star at its rising, they followed that star wherever it went. We don't have to look to a star to guide us to the truth; we have the truth in Jesus.

I learned something else from that NASA scientist involved with the Hubble Space Telescope: the galaxies are moving. Our Milky Way galaxy is on a collision course with another galaxy, Andromeda. The two galaxies are projected to collide in about four billion years. It sounds shocking, but apparently such cosmic collisions take place all the time.

Two thousand years ago heaven came to earth in the birth of baby. It was a cosmic collision that has changed the course of human destiny. God came to us, and we have seen his glory—the glory of the Father's only Son, full of grace and truth. No one has ever seen God. It is the Son, the way, the truth, the life, who has made him known.

QUESTIONS FOR DISCUSSION/REFLECTION

1. Who were the wise men, and what made them wise?
2. What motivated the wise men to make such a long journey?
3. Why did the wise men bring gifts? What gifts would you bring?
4. How do you think the experience changed the wise men?
5. What is the meaning of this story for your life?

NOTE

[1]Steve Agnew, quoted in "One in five Americans reports no religious affiliation, study says," by Michelle Boorstein, WashingtonPost.com, Oct. 9, 2012.

CHAPTER 4

JOSEPH HAD A DREAM
(Matt. 2:13-23)

> *An angel from the Lord appeared to Joseph in a dream and said, "Get up. Take the child and his mother and escape to Egypt." After King Herod died, an angel from the Lord appeared in a dream to Joseph in Egypt. "Get up," the angel said, "and take the child and his mother and go to the land of Israel."*
>
> (Matt. 2:13a, 19-20a CEB)

This is not a Christmas story. It explains how Jesus escaped the massacre of male children in Bethlehem, and how he ended up in Nazareth. The story stands in stark contrast to the joy of the night when Jesus was born, and the peace on earth the angels had sung about. Matthew saw the holy family's escape to Egypt, and their eventual return to the land of Israel, as the fulfillment of an ancient prophesy in Hosea 11:1. Matthew also saw the murder of the young boys in Bethlehem as the fulfillment of a prophecy in Jeremiah 31:15. Rachel, the beloved wife of Jacob and mother of Joseph and Benjamin, died in childbirth, and was buried near Bethlehem (Gen. 35:16-19). Ramah, where Jeremiah was freed to remain in Judah rather than being exiled to Babylon, became a symbol of national grief (Jer. 40:1).

This story in Matthew is filled with theological conundrums. Jesus was saved, but the other boys in Bethlehem were not. God warned Joseph in a dream, but what about the other parents in Bethlehem? Were they not warned too? Herod acted according to his character. He was well known for his ruthless cruelty. After Herod died in 4 BC, he was succeeded by Archelaus, who was almost as vicious as his father. Once again God to spoke to Joseph in a dream.

MASSACRE OF THE INNOCENTS
(Matt. 2:13-18)

The story of the murder of young males as decreed by Herod is one of the most difficult stories in the Bible. An angel of the Lord appeared to Joseph in a dream and told him to flee to Egypt with the infant Jesus and his mother. The angel warned that Herod was about to search for the child to destroy him. Joseph did as he was told. Under the cover of darkness, the family fled Bethlehem and traveled south to Egypt, where there were Jewish communities in almost every city. There they remained in exile until Herod died. The good news is that Jesus was spared. The bad news is that the other babies left behind in Bethlehem did not escape Herod's wrath. Every male child under the age of two in and around Bethlehem was slaughtered.

Such a massacre of innocents was in character for King Herod. He raised cruelty to a whole new level. Married 10 times, Herod divorced, dismissed, or simply ignored most of his wives once he grew tired of them. As for his favorite wife, Herod eventually murdered her. He also killed (or had killed) his uncle, his brother, his son-in-law, his mother-in-law, and three of his favorite sons. Because Herod was only half Jewish and had won the crown through violence and collusion with Rome, he was paranoid about possible rivals to his throne. Rome had installed him as king of the Jews in 37 BC, and Rome tolerated his viciousness only because Herod levied oppressive taxes on the Jewish people and ruthlessly suppressed any potential rebellion.

Near the end of his life, Herod rounded up some citizens and had them arrested on false charges. His sole purpose was to order that they be killed upon his death. Biblical commentator William Barclay noted that Herod "was well aware that no one would mourn his death, and he was determined that some tears should be shed when he died." Given that mentality, massacring the infants in and around Bethlehem was no big deal. Bethlehem was a small community, and the total number of children killed was probably less than 20. Herod was so infuriated that he had been tricked by the wise men that he did not care about the innocent lives lost or the suffering of those 20 families.

Children have always been vulnerable to political forces. The United Nations reports that half of the world's refugees are children. Those children are at risk of abuse, violence, neglect, exploitation, trafficking, and forced military conscription. And it's not just overseas. Unaccompanied children and youth have poured into the United States from Mexico and Central America. Thousands have come from El Salvador, Guate-mala, and Honduras, which according to the Center for American Progress, are "three of the five most dangerous countries in the world." The children are fleeing violence from drug cartels, street gangs, and other criminal organizations. These unaccompanied minors entering the U.S. from Central America do not include the thousands of Mexican children sent back to Mexico after only a day or two in U.S. custody. This so-called "illegal immigration" has become a major political issue.

How easily we forget that Jesus was a child refugee, fleeing from violence in his country. He was not an unaccompanied minor when he crossed the border into Egypt, but Jesus was a refugee. Had Jesus not fled from Bethlehem with his parents, he likely would have been killed along with the other children.

According to the United Nations, many millions of children have been displaced by violence and other hardships. We have heard about the refugee crisis in Syria, and the tens of thousands of refugees pouring into surrounding countries and trying to make their way to Europe. But there are refugee crises in Asia and Africa also. UNICEF reports that some 1.4 million children in Nigeria have been displaced by the violence of Boko Haram. Millions more have been displaced by violence in South Sudan. There are modern-day "Herods" in many countries around the world, and children are the most vulnerable of their victims. Refugees and massacres are not just ancient history; they are a part of our present reality.

Tragically, we have experienced the massacre of innocent people in the United States. Many of them have been children and young people. We will never forget when a lone gunman in Newtown, Connecticut slaughtered 20 children and six adults at Sandy Hook Elementary School. A few years before that a lone gunman killed 32 students and teachers at Virginia Tech University. Both of those killers apparently were inspired by the Columbine shooters in Colorado who killed 12 of their fellow students and a teacher. More recently a lone gunman killed nine innocent people during a Bible study in a church in Charleston, South Carolina. Then a lone gunman killed 8 students and a teacher at Umpqua Community College in Oregon and wounded 9 others. Then a married couple killed 14 and wounded 22 others at a holiday party in San Bernardino, California. The Anti-Defamation League's Center on Extremism has identified four movements behind such massacres: white supremacy, anti-government extremism, domestic Islamist extremism, and anti-abortion extremism. In addition, there are troubled individuals who kill for no known reason.

Tragically, the massacre of innocents in Bethlehem did not stop with Bethlehem. There have been many other massacres of innocents down through the centuries, and each time the words of the prophet Jeremiah are fulfilled: "A voice was heard in Ramah, wailing and loud lamentation, Rachel weeping for her children; she refused to be consoled, because they are no more."

Rachel, the beloved wife of Jacob, died in childbirth and was buried in Bethlehem (Genesis 35). Ramah, north of Jerusalem, was a place of national grief (Jer. 40:1) and a transit point for deportees to exile in Babylon. Jeremiah depicts Rachel, the mother of Joseph and Benjamin, lamenting from the grave the loss of innocent lives. Her wails are heard as far as Ramah. The point is that any loss of innocent lives is a tragedy. "Rachel weeping for her children" is a sign that all of heaven weeps when even one innocent life is lost.

We might wonder, if God saved Jesus from the destruction of King Herod, why didn't God save all the other babies in Bethlehem? Why didn't God save the children in Sandy Hook Elementary School, or the young adults at Virginia Tech, or the students at Columbine High School, or the faithful Christians at Emmanuel AME Church in Charleston, or the workers at the office holiday party in San Bernardino, California? Why does God intervene in some situations, but not in others? Simply put, we do not know. We cannot know the mind of God. But we do know that God cares.

Tragedies happen because God has given us freedom. Sometimes humans misuse that freedom to do terrible things to others. It must break God's heart to see us hurting, abusing, and killing each other. From the beginning, God has wanted us to be in right relationship with him and and with our fellow humans and the rest of creation. But sin has repeatedly disrupted those relationships. We live in a fallen world, and violence against one another is tragic evidence of our sinful condition. But God has never given up on us. In the fullness of time, God sent his Son Jesus to forgive us, and to redeem us, and to call us back to himself. Jesus was spared from the massacre at Bethlehem, but that was so he could become the sacrifice for our sins. As Paul wrote, "God did not spare his own Son, but gave him up for us all" (Rom. 8:32).

God so loved the world that he gave his only Son, not just to be born in a manger, but to die on a cross. When we accept Jesus as our Savior by faith, we are made right with

God. But that does not automatically make everything right with the world. When Jesus was born, the angels sang about peace on earth and goodwill among people, but we have a part to play in that. Peace and goodwill do not just happen because Jesus was born, but as a result of people who have been saved by faith putting their faith into action and working to make peace and goodwill a reality in the world.

So, we have a part to play in God's work in the world. We can pray that God's will may be done on earth as it is in heaven, but we also can take actions to promote God's will on earth. We can make decisions and take actions to promote peace and challenge injustice, to show compassion for refugees, and to seek to limit those who would cause harm to others. We may not be able to prevent every massacre, but surely, we can reduce their frequency. Surely, we can do something to curtail the violence and to advance peace and understanding. Surely, we can do something about the refugee crisis, immigration, and gun violence, and limit those who would cause harm to their fellow human beings. We have a lot of work yet to do for God's will to be done on earth.

Rachel is still weeping for her children. Heaven weeps when any innocent life is lost. As people of faith, let us put our faith into action and press our representatives in government to take action to reduce violence and promote peace. Jesus said, "Blessed are the peacemakers, for they will be called children of God" (Matt. 5:9). Oh Lord, lead us to peace.

TRAGEDY AND CONSOLATION
(Matt. 2:13-18)

Melissa d'Arabian is a television personality on the Food Network. She is a wife, the mother of four daughters, and the author of a bestselling cookbook, *Ten Dollar Dinners*. In addition to hosting her own cooking show, she has appeared on various other Food Network primetime series, and she is a sought-after speaker and contributing writer for print and online publications. But life was not always so good for Melissa.

The child of a single mother, Melissa grew up poor in Tucson, Arizona. Melissa says she was raised in a humble home "with a coupon-cutter mentality and on a shoestring budget . . . where waste was never a temptation." An elementary school secretary recognized Melissa was in need and made sure that she got enough nutritious food to eat and connected her family with government-assistance programs. Eventually the family moved to Maryland, and Melissa was able to attend the University of Vermont where she majored in political science. But while she was still an undergraduate student, a tragic event happened that would forever change her life.

It happened in 1989, when Melissa was a 20-year-old college student. One evening during the spring semester she called home to Maryland to talk with her mother. It was no big deal; Melissa just needed her mother's credit card number so she could register for a graduate exam prep course. But when someone answered the phone at her home, it was not her mother. It was an unfamiliar male voice. He identified himself as an officer with the police department. They had a short conversation Melissa would never forget. The officer informed Melissa that her mother had died, by apparent suicide. Needless to say, Melissa was devastated—emotionally, financially, relationally, spiritually, and in almost every other way. Her mother's untimely death, and in such a tragic manner, crushed her spirit. The tragedy shook the very foundation of her life. Her mother's suicide plunged Melissa into a decade-long crisis of faith. It took almost 25 years for her to come to the point where she was able to use the platform of her celebrity to talk about it.[1]

A tragic event can alter the course of a person's life. Jackie Kennedy was never the same after her husband, President John Kennedy, was assassinated in 1963. She lived another 30-plus years after her husband was killed, but she was never able to completely get over it. After she moved out of the executive mansion but was still living in the city of Washington, Mrs. Kennedy asked her Secret Service drivers to avoid routes that might cause her to see the White House. The memories were just too painful. She returned to the White House only once more the rest of her life. She and her children made a secret, un-photographed visit in 1971 to see the official portraits of her and the late president. She later wrote to President Nixon, thanking him for his hospitality: "A day I had always dreaded turned out to be one of the most precious ones I have spent with my children."

After Bill Clinton was elected president, First Lady Hillary Rodham Clinton invited her good friend Jackie to revisit the White House in 1993. Jackie appreciated the gesture but declined the invitation. After his mother died the following year, John Kennedy Jr. wrote to Mrs. Clinton to explain: "Since she left Washington, I believe she resisted ever connecting with it emotionally . . . it had much to do with the memories stirred."

For most people, the loss of a loved one causes pain and grief. But when the loss is sudden or unexpected or tragic, the grief can be so intense that it never seems to go away. Sometimes the grief even intensifies over time. Mental health professions call such a reaction "complicated grief." It is estimated that about 10 percent of people who suffer a significant loss experience complicated grief. Those who lose a loved one by suicide are more likely to experience complicated grief. So are those who lose a loved one to violence. So are parents who lose a child. That is the situation of our scripture passage.

It is a story with two sides. First, there is the happy side. The infant Jesus was spared the wrath of King Herod when Joseph fled with the child and his mother to Egypt. Having been warned by an angel in a dream that Herod was about to search for the child to destroy him, Joseph took action. He left in the middle of the night and traveled as far as was necessary to escape Herod's murderous rage. The family would remain in Egypt until Herod died. That is the good part of the story.

The sad part of the story is what happened to the boy babies who remained in Bethlehem. Herod ordered that all of them under the age of two be indiscriminately killed. It was their parents' worst nightmare. We don't know exactly how many children died, but even one would be too many. William Barclay estimates that the village of Bethlehem might have had 20 to 30 boys under the age of two. It sounds unbelievably cruel, but Herod had a reputation for brutality. Barclay says, "Herod was a past master in the art of assassination." Shortly after he came to the throne, he annihilated members of the Sanhedrin, the ruling court of the Jews. Later he slaughtered 300 court officers. Still later in 7 BC he had his wife Mariamne murdered, along with her mother Alexandra, his eldest son Antipater, and two other sons, Alexander and Aristobulus. Given that record, it's not surprising that Herod would order the slaughter of the innocents in Bethlehem to eliminate any potential new rival to his throne. The surprising part of the story is not that many innocent children were killed, for that was totally in keeping with Herod's character and past conduct. The surprising part of the story is that the family of Jesus managed to escape the destruction.

Still, even though Jesus escaped, Matthew recognizes the tragic nature of what happened. The infant Jesus was spared, but many other babies and their families were not spared. Matthew saw the killing of the boys in Bethlehem as fulfillment of a prophecy in Jeremiah. It was not that God wanted the children to die. Violence against the innocent children of Bethlehem was the last thing God wanted. But God has given humans freedom, even the freedom to do terrible wrong. God does not intervene to stop the terrible wrong, because to intervene would be to negate human freedom. So, savage men such as Herod commit murder, and children and their families suffer unspeakable loss. But God is not unmoved.

The prophet Jeremiah expressed the anguish of lamentation, describing it as "Rachel weeping for her children." Rachel was the wife of the Old Testament patriarch Jacob, who died centuries before Jeremiah wrote his prophecy. In describing the destruction of Jerusalem by the Babylonians, Jeremiah said that long-departed Rachel was weeping for her children, even from the grave. Matthew saw this prophecy as an apt description of the murder of the innocents in Bethlehem. Rachel was once again weeping for her children. Jeremiah said, "she refused to be consoled because they are no more" (Matt. 2:18b). In the tragedy in Bethlehem, Rachel weeps for her children—and God weeps too.

What Matthew describes is complicated grief. It's a grief that "refuses to be consoled." It's a grief that won't go away, even with the passage of time. For most people, when they lose a loved one, the pain is intense at first, but then, slowly, over time, they find a way to move on. But with complicated grief, those who are bereaved cannot seem to get past it. The grief goes on and on.

In 2004, after her son died of bone cancer at the age of 13, Stephanie Muldberg "refused to be consoled." She remained stuck in her mourning, staring aimlessly out the window, sleeping little some nights, staying in bed some days, crying, and crying, and crying some more. Stephanie says, "Every day was a chore. My first thought each morning was, 'When will all this end?'" She stopped answering the phone. She turned down invitations to go out with friends. After a while, her confused and frustrated friends stopped inviting her to go out. Stephanie withdrew more and more into an isolation she had imposed upon herself. Finally, after many months of prolonged grieving, Stephanie got some help. She agreed to participate in a psychotherapy intervention program with a therapist who specialized in complicated grief.

Stephanie's treatment involved sessions in which she revisited the moment of her son's death and carried on an imaginary conversation with him. She told her son how sad and angry she was that he suffered so much, especially from the bone surgery late in his treatment. In doing that, she finally began to let go of the guilt that she had not done enough, or that she had done the wrong things to try to help her son. Now, having completed the program, Stephanie considers her grief to be integrated and healthy. She says, "It never goes away because the loss never goes away." But now she can drive past the athletic fields where her son used to play baseball, and she can remember "the joy of life with him." The overwhelming sorrow is gradually being replaced with good memories, and that has given Stephanie hope to go on.[2]

It took Melissa d'Arabian a long time to get her life back after her mother committed suicide. Getting married and having children helped. So did her television career and engaging in causes she is passionate about. First, Melissa got involved in a campaign to fight children's hunger, and then she began volunteering with the American Foundation for Suicide Prevention. Because she knows firsthand how suicide affects a family, she is speaking out about her own story. In so doing she is seeking to help prevent suicide as a way to honor her mom and to help those who have been left behind. Most of all, Melissa relies on her Christian faith to live with meaning and purpose.

Jesus was spared the sword of King Herod for a purpose. His purpose was to grow up to become the Savior of humankind; to seek and to save the lost; to heal the broken-hearted; to proclaim release to the captives. The meaning of his life is that all who are weary from carrying heavy burdens can find rest for their souls. There is hope beyond the heartache. The love of God is greater than the tragedies of life. Yes, grief eventually will come to everyone, but God is greater than our grief.

Who can separate us from the love of Christ . . . tribulation or distress, persecution or famine, tragedy or death? No, in all these things we are more than conquerors through him who loved us. Nothing can separate us from the love of God in Christ Jesus our Lord. This promise from Romans 8 is our peace; it is our consolation. Nothing is greater than God.

FOLLOW YOUR DREAM
(Matt. 2:19-23)

It was one of the most famous speeches in American history. On August 28, 1963, Martin Luther King Jr. stood on the steps of the Lincoln Memorial and spoke to perhaps a quarter-million people gathered around the reflecting pool on the National Mall, and to a national television audience. In his 17-minute address, Rev. Dr. King called for an end to racism in America. He called for a new era of freedom, justice, equality, and opportunity. His address was the closing speech in an historic public demonstration called the "March on Washington for Jobs and Freedom."

Many people are too young to remember, but in 1963 our society was radically segregated. Racial minorities were discriminated against in many ways. Most schools were separate and unequal. Most houses of worship were not racially diverse. Economic opportunities for minorities were limited. In many places unjust laws amounted to legalized discrimination. African Americans could be refused service at restaurants, theaters, motels, doctors' offices, and other places of business. I can remember seeing signs hanging in store windows: "We reserve the right to refuse service to anyone." Many residential communities were also segregated.

In 1963 I was in junior high school (now called middle school). I did not have any African-American classmates until I was in high school. The only African Americans I knew growing up were the lady who cleaned our house and my grandmother's house once a week, and employees at the laundry and dry-cleaning plant where I worked after school and on Saturdays. I had some Jewish friends and a few Asian-American and Hispanic friends, but I did not have any African-American friends my age until I went to college. My how things have changed since Martin Luther King gave his "I Have a Dream" speech on the steps of the Lincoln Memorial!

The basic premise of King's speech was that he dreamed of a better day. He dreamed of a time when people would be judged not by the color of their skin but by the content of their character. Quoting the scriptures, he dreamed of a day when justice would roll down like waters and righteousness like a mighty stream. This was revolutionary stuff in 1963. In fact, following that historic event at the Lincoln Memorial, the FBI expanded its investigation of King and the Southern Christian Leadership Conference he led. The day after the "I Have a Dream" speech, Special Agent William Sullivan, who was heading the FBI investigation, wrote this in a memo:

> In the light of King's powerful demagogic speech yesterday, he stands head and shoulders above all other Negro leaders put together when it comes to influencing the great masses of Negroes. We must mark him now, if we have not done so before, as the most dangerous Negro of the future in this nation from the standpoint of communism, the Negro, and national security.

After the speech, the FBI ramped up its investigation of King, aiming to smear and discredit him. But within a few months of the speech, he was named *Time* magazine's "Man of the Year." The following year he was awarded the Nobel Peace Prize, the youngest person ever so honored. And it all started with a dream.

In our scripture passage, Joseph was guided by a dream. He was guided by a series of dreams, to be exact. First, he was guided by a dream to leave Bethlehem with Mary and Jesus and flee to Egypt to escape the murderous wrath of King Herod. Next, he was guided by a dream to leave Egypt after Herod had died and return to the land of Israel. Finally, he was guided by a dream to settle the family in Nazareth, since Herod's son Archelaus had succeeded his father and was still a threat in Bethlehem. In the case of Joseph, his dreams seem to have been literal nighttime dreams that occurred when he was asleep. In those dreams an angel of the Lord appeared to Joseph and guided him to what he was to do.

Martin Luther King's dream was not so much a nighttime visitation of an angel as much as it was a daytime vision of what God would have him to do. But no less than Joseph, King was convinced that his dream was inspired by God. As a Baptist minister, he had spent his life studying the scriptures. He was convinced that God loves all people and wants them to be free. A dream can be a powerful thing. A dream can change a person's life, or even the life of a nation.

A few years ago, U.S. Supreme Court Justice Sonia Sotomayor released her deeply personal memoir, *My Beloved World.* Only the third woman and the first Latina to serve on the Supreme Court, Sotomayor is the embodiment of the American dream. She was born to immigrants from Puerto Rico and raised in a Spanish-speaking home in the housing projects of the Bronx, New York. She was diagnosed with Type 1 diabetes at the age of 8 and not given much hope for a long life. Her alcoholic father died when she was 9, leaving her mother to raise Sonia and her younger brother alone. Her mother dreamed of a better life for her children.

Even though she barely earned enough money to keep a roof over their heads, her mother bought a set of *Encyclopedia Britannica* books for Sonia and her brother. In the sixth grade, after watching an episode of the *Perry Mason* show on television, Sonia dreamed of one day becoming a judge. It seemed an improbable dream for a sickly, poor, underprivileged Hispanic girl from the Bronx, being raised by a single mother who hardly spoke English. But Sonia applied herself in school and won a scholarship to Princeton under Affirmative Action.

When Sonia got to college, she realized how unprepared she was, compared to students from more privileged backgrounds. Even though she was raised in the Bronx, she had not dared to venture into Manhattan until she was in high school. Many of her classmates at Princeton had been exposed to so much more of the world than she had. At first she worried that she was not as smart as her fellow students at the elite Ivy League school. When a classmate mentioned *Alice in Wonderland*, Sonia asked, "Alice who?" Then she came to realize that many of the gaps in her knowledge and understanding were not because she was intellectually inferior. Rather, it was simply because of the limitations of her cultural background.

Sonia had a data-entry job at Princeton as a part of her scholarship. As she was inputting financial records for some of her fellow students, she got her first introduction to trust funds and tax write-offs and complex financial instruments. This was for a girl whose family did not even have a bank account. In her memoir she wrote: "I honestly felt no envy or resentment, only astonishment at how much of a world there was out there and how much of it others already knew. The agenda for self-cultivation that had been set for my classmates by their teachers and parents was something I'd have to develop for myself."

During her freshman year Sonia realized that her writing skills needed improvement. Her English was riddled with Spanish constructions and colloquialisms. Sonia decided she would have to work on her own to catch up with the other students, so she bought grammar and vocabulary texts and studied each lunch hour during her summer job. When she returned to Princeton for her sophomore year, her grades began to improve. By the time she graduated with highest honors, *summa cum laude*, Sonia Sotomayor had won Princeton's top academic prize. The irony is that Sonia did not even know what the Latin phrase *summa cum laude* meant. She had to look it up!

After Princeton, Sonia was offered a scholarship to Yale Law School, again under Affirmative Action. She later said she felt no reason to apologize that the admissions policies of Princeton and Yale had opened doors for her. She recognized that was the purpose: "to create the conditions whereby students from disadvantaged backgrounds could be brought to the starting line of a race many were unaware was even being run."[3]

Sonia Sotomayor followed her dream of one day being a judge, and now she is a justice on the highest court in the land. Joseph followed his dreams and saved the infant

Jesus from the murderous rage of King Herod and the threats of Herod's son. Martin Luther King Jr. followed his dream of a country that could see beyond race and provide equal opportunity to all. A dream can change a person's life. A dream can even change the life of a nation.

No matter your age, you can follow God's dream for your life. You can follow your deepest dream, which if you believe in Jesus and seek to follow Jesus, is also God's dream for your life. May God help you to dream big, and to follow that dream, that you might do the things and become the person for which he has called you.

QUESTIONS FOR DISCUSSION/REFLECTION

1. Have you ever thought about Jesus being a refugee? How does his early situation affect your thoughts about refugees today?
2. How do you square the "massacre of the innocents" with the love of God?
3. What does this story tell us about respect for human life?
4. Has God ever spoken to you in a dream? If so, how did you know it was God speaking? Did you act on God's message?
5. Jesus was saved for a purpose. For what purpose have you been saved?

NOTES

[1]Melissa d'Arabian's story is told in *Parade*, Nov. 3, 2013.
[2]Stephanie Muldberg's story is told in *Parade*, Oct. 27, 2013.
[3]Sonia Sotomayor's story is told in her memoir, *My Beloved World* (Vintage Books, 2013).

CHAPTER 5

ZECHARIAH AND ELIZABETH
(Luke 1:5-25)

"Don't be afraid, Zechariah. Your prayers have been heard. Your wife Elizabeth will give birth to your son and you must name him John. Many people will rejoice at his birth, for he will be great in the Lord's eyes… What I have spoken will come true at the proper time."
(Luke 1:13-15a, 20a CEB)

Zechariah was a priest when Herod was king, which means that the story about Zechariah and Elizabeth took place sometime between 40 BC and 4 BC, because those were the years when Herod was king of the Jews. Zechariah was a godly man, married to a godly woman named Elizabeth. Both were descendants of Aaron, the brother of Moses. (Note: this is not the Old Testament prophet Zechariah who lived in the 6th century BC and after whom a book in the Old Testament is named. Zechariah the priest came along six centuries later.)

By virtue of his ancestry, Zechariah was a priest. This sounds like an honor, but to put things in perspective, the country was crawling with priests. Every direct descendant of Aaron was automatically a priest. Scholars estimate that there were as many as 20,000 priests in Judea at that time. There were not enough jobs in the Temple to keep so many priests employed. So, these priests were divided into 24 divisions, and each division served in the Temple two weeks of the year. But even then, there were too many priests for each one to have something to do. So, they drew lots to see which priest would get to fulfill a ceremonial role during the appointed week.

Zechariah won the lottery, and this once-in-a-lifetime honor would be his. But Zechariah got far more than he had bargained for. He received news that would change his life, and the life of his wife Elizabeth. They were both very old, but Elizabeth would have a child. No wonder Zechariah was speechless. There was more important work for this couple to do.

WHAT THE LORD HAS DONE
(Luke 1:5-14, 18-20, 24-25)

Sometimes people do not deserve what life gives them. Zechariah and Elizabeth did not deserve what life gave them. They were good people. Luke tells us they were "righteous before God, living blamelessly according to all the commandments and regulations of the Lord." They came from good families. Both were descendants of Aaron. Yet, they had no children. In their day, for a couple to be childless was seen as a curse.

Who would bring laughter into their home? Who would give them a greater purpose beyond themselves? Who would take care of them in their old age? Who would carry on the family lineage?

A couple without children was seen to be a disgrace. Surely, Zechariah and Elizabeth had done something wrong to deserve such a fate. Yet, it wasn't their fault. Elizabeth's barrenness was not a punishment from God. It was a condition that God would use to grow their faith, and to do a great thing.

In our day, it is difficult to understand why Elizabeth would have felt such disgrace. Today we recognize value in a woman beyond her childbearing potential. A woman can have a career, pursue her ambitions, and have a full and meaningful life without children. There is no stigma for a woman to be childless, but in biblical times there was a stigma. A woman's primary purpose in life was to bear children and to take care of her husband. If a woman did not have children, she was looked upon with disdain—even disgrace. Such was the condition of Elizabeth. We can only imagine the anguish she and Zechariah felt, thinking that somehow life and even God had passed them by. They were both getting on in years and seemingly without hope.

Then, suddenly, unexpectedly, their lot changed. Zechariah was chosen to offer incense in the Temple. This was a great honor. Although Zechariah was a priest, he was one of many. There were thousands of "country priests" in Palestine. The priests were organized into 24 divisions, with each division serving in the Temple for one week twice per year. From each division, priests were chosen by lot during their assigned week to participate in Temple rituals for a day. On this day, the lot fell to Zechariah. This was a once-in-a-lifetime opportunity. Many priests were never given the opportunity to offer incense. And after his time had passed, Zechariah would never be selected to offer incense in the Temple again.

Zechariah must have been filled with emotion. What a story he would have to tell his wife Elizabeth! Finally, after all those years of disappointment, something had gone right in his life. As worshippers were praying outside in the courtyard, Zechariah entered the Temple and stood in the Holy Place. Before him was the curtain of the Temple, and behind the curtain, the Holy of Holies. Zechariah could not enter the Holy of Holies, but he could stand in the Holy Place beside the table of shewbread. To his right was the golden candlestick, and directly in front of him was the golden altar of incense. It must have been the spiritual high point of Zechariah's life. But suddenly his exhilaration turned to terror.

An angel of the Lord appeared beside the altar. When Zechariah saw the angel, he was overwhelmed with fear. But the angel said, "Don't be afraid, Zechariah, for your prayer has been heard. Your wife Elizabeth will bear a son; you will name him John." Zechariah was stunned. How could this be? He was an old man, and his wife was getting on in years. The angel replied, "I am Gabriel ... sent to bring you this good news. But since you did not believe my words, you will become mute, unable to speak, until the day these things occur."

When Zechariah finally emerged from the Holy Place, the people waiting outside had been wondering about the delay. Seeing he was mute and could not speak, they surmised he had seen a vision in the sanctuary. He gestured to them, but he could not utter a word. When Zechariah returned home the promise came true. Elizabeth conceived. After all those years of waiting she was with child. For five months she remained in seclusion. Finally, Elizabeth proclaimed: "This is what the Lord has done for me. He looked favorably upon me and took away the disgrace I endured."

The angel had told Zechariah that he and Elizabeth would have a son, and they were to name him John. The name John in Hebrew, *Yohanan*, means "God has been gracious," or "God has shown favor." Zechariah and Elizabeth's son would grow up to be John the Baptist, who would prepare the way for Jesus. Shortly after Elizabeth emerged from her five months of seclusion, her cousin Mary became pregnant by the Holy Spirit. Pregnant Mary came to visit pregnant Elizabeth. When Elizabeth heard Mary's greeting, the child in Elizabeth's womb leaped for joy, and Elizabeth was filled with the Holy Spirit. So, even before he was born, John was announcing the coming Messiah, through his mother Elizabeth!

What are we to make of this remarkable story? Well, for one thing, it is a story about patient faith. When life did not go the way Zechariah and Elizabeth wanted, they never gave up their faith in God. They never stopped believing. Year after year, they remained childless. Year after year, they endured the disgrace of their people. Yet, they never stopped praying, and they never gave up hope. People of lesser faith might have become disillusioned or angry or bitter, but Zechariah and Elizabeth remained faithful. People of lesser faith might have turned away from God, but for Zechariah and Elizabeth, their years of disappointment and suffering did not alienate them from God. Instead, they had drawn closer to God. Finally, their faith was rewarded and God answered their prayers.

Sometimes, when life does not go our way, we are tempted to question or doubt God or even to give up on God. Zechariah and Elizabeth are examples of patient faith. Difficult circumstances are not God's punishment; they are opportunities for God to grow our faith and to do a great thing.

We also can learn from this story that God's timing and our timing are not always the same. Year after year Zechariah and Elizabeth had longed for a child, but no child was given. But in the fullness of time, God's will was done. After greeting her cousin Mary, Elizabeth came to realize that the child Elizabeth had been given after all those years of waiting could not have come any sooner. Her son would have to be born exactly when he was in order to fulfill his role in God's plan. Because John would prepare the way for Jesus, the timing of his birth was critical. Only in her old age could Elizabeth become the mother of the prophet who would prepare the way of the Lord.

Sometimes life doesn't seem to unfold according to our timetable. Sometimes we wonder why God is taking so long. Sometimes it is only in retrospect, only in looking back, that we can recognize how God's hand was at work in our lives. In Romans 8:28 Paul wrote, "We know that all things work together for good for those who love God." Paul did not say that all things are good. Some things in our lives are not good. Pain, suffering, illness, heartache, loneliness, and loss are not good. But God works in all things. God can use the hard things of life to draw us closer to himself.

Lacey Dunkin had always dreamed of becoming a mother. Yet, when she was in her mid-20s and living with her parents, she wondered if that dream would ever come true. Lacey had no prospect of marriage. There was no man in her life. At her mother's suggestion, Lacey applied with a family services agency to become a foster parent. After completing a series of classes and passing a home study, Lacey was certified in June of 2011. Nothing happened for several months—no calls, no contacts. By September, Lacey worried that as a single woman she might never be contacted. Then, late one night, a social worker called about an emergency foster care placement. Four sisters—ages 5, 2-year-old twins, and a 1-year-old baby—needed a home. Could Lacey take them in?

Lacey was not prepared to take four young children all at once, but she said yes. Within a couple of hours, there were four frightened and confused little girls running around her living room. Lacey and her mother calmed the tired and crying girls as they tucked them into bed. Lacey rocked the baby to sleep. The next morning Lacey called in to work and told them she would not be able to make it that day. Instead, she would be taking the 5-year-old to kindergarten. While making her breakfast, the little girl asked Lacey if she could be her daughter. It broke Lacey's heart. By the time they got to school, the little girl was introducing Lacey as her mom.

Later that day Lacey learned that the four little girls had a sister, born the night before. The baby would be placed in a foster home with a couple who had prior experience with newborns. Lacey took care of the four older sisters for nine months. Then the birth mother regained custody, and the girls went to live with her. Once again, Lacey's heart was broken. Lacey said, "I tried to keep faith that they would end up where they were supposed to be, and in my heart, that was here [with me]."

About a month later, the girls' birth mother decided that she could not take care of them. She called Lacey and asked if Lacey would take all five. Lacey formally adopted all five girls in July of 2013. The girls asked Lacey if she was sure they were staying. Lacey said, "You're adopted. You're home forever." Then there was one more surprise. The birth mother was expecting again. It was another girl, born in September. Eventually that baby came to live with Lacey, and she was adopted, too.

Lacey's prayers to become a mother were answered in a way that she never could have imagined. Lacey said, "You don't set out to have six little girls. [But] I'm glad that it happened. I'm so blessed."[1]

God can use the circumstances of any life to grow our faith and to do a great thing. Just ask Zechariah and Elizabeth or Lacey Dunkin. There is no telling what the Lord can do.

HOPE
(Luke 1:5-17)

As a kid, I loved baseball. I loved watching it, and I loved playing it. I told my friend Rix Quinn that when I grew up, I wanted to become a professional baseball player. Rix just laughed at me, but I was serious. That was my ambition in life, to play major league baseball. There were only two problems: I wasn't very big, and I wasn't very good. I played second base on my Little League baseball team. I think I batted seventh or eighth in the lineup. That tells you what kind of hitter I was. I was a little better in the field than I was at the plate, but I certainly was not the star of our team. So, my hopes of becoming a professional baseball player were never realized.

I loved watching baseball on television and listening to games on the radio. My favorite teams were the St. Louis Cardinals and the New York Yankees. We didn't have any major league baseball teams in Texas back then. The Washington Senators would move and become the Texas Rangers in 1972, but I was away at college by then. So, St. Louis was the closest team to Fort Worth, and I liked the Yankees because of Mickey Mantle and Yogi Berra. I also was a fan of Willie Mays, but the Cardinals and the Yankees were my favorite major league teams.

My favorite minor league baseball team was the Fort Worth Cats. Rix's father, Bill Quinn, used to take us to see the Cats play at the old LaGrave field on the north side of town. Rix and I would always take our baseball gloves to the games, hoping to catch a foul ball. If you caught a baseball, you got to keep it. I don't know how many times we saw the Fort Worth Cats play over the years, but every time we went to a game, we took our gloves. Neither Rix nor I ever caught a foul ball—never even came close—but we lived in hope that one day a ball would come our way.

In our scripture passage, Zechariah and Elizabeth also lived in hope—in hope for a child. The problem was, both were getting up in years, and Elizabeth was barren. We may not understand what a crisis that was, because women have so many options today. Not every woman wants to have a child in our time. But in ancient times, a woman's primary role in life was to become a mother. A woman without children was almost a woman without purpose. A man without children was equally desperate. Without an heir, a man would have no way to perpetuate his name and no way to leave a legacy after he was gone. So, for both Elizabeth and Zechariah, being without a child was a pitiable condition. To make matters worse, it seemed so unfair. They were good people; if anyone deserved children, it was Elizabeth and Zechariah. Luke described them as "righteous before God, living blamelessly according to all the commandments and regulations of the law." Yet, God had not blessed them with children. It's hard to maintain your faith when you seem to be doing everything right and still things don't happen the way you want them to.

Not only were they righteous and living blamelessly, but Zechariah also was a priest. He had devoted his life to God. And Elizabeth was a godly woman, a descendant of a priestly order. Serving God was in this couple's blood. They had no children, but they remained faithful. In spite of their bitter disappointment, they continued to do what they believed God wanted them to do. Life had not turned out the way they had hoped, but they continued to do the right things and to live the right way. It might have been tempting for them to turn away from God, since God had seemingly turned away from them and deprived them of children. But their relationship with God was not based on "what's in it for me." Their relationship with God was based on faith. They remained faithful to God because they believed God would remain faithful to them. They didn't know how things would turn out, but they kept trusting and believing and hoping in faith.

While Zechariah was fulfilling his commitment as a priest in the Temple, an angel of the Lord appeared to him. Naturally, Zechariah was terrified. He never imagined that offering incense to the Lord would draw the Lord's attention. Sure, he and his wife had prayed for a child. But never in his wildest dreams did he expect God to answer their prayers in such a direct way. The angel said, "Don't be afraid, Zechariah, for your prayer has been heard. Your wife Elizabeth will bear you a son and you will name him John. You will have joy and gladness, and many will rejoice at his birth, for he will be great in the sight of the Lord."

The promise would come true. Elizabeth would become pregnant, even in her old age, and she would bear a son. He would become great in the sight of the Lord, for John would grow up to be John the Baptist, who would prepare the way for the Messiah. Zechariah and Elizabeth would receive even more than they had hoped for. Sometimes God answers our prayers in ways we could have never imagined.

This is a story not only about the conception of John the Baptist, but also a story about the faithfulness of God and of Zechariah and Elizabeth. The childless couple remained faithful to God even when it seemed their prayers would not be answered. They kept hoping, even when it seemed that the years were going to pass them by and leave them childless and bereft. They remained faithful, not to be rewarded, but because they had faith. They lived in hope even when life was hard. And in the end, they were rewarded for their faithfulness with the gift of a son.

One Thanksgiving afternoon, while many people were hunkered down in front of the television set watching football and others were having a third helping of turkey and dressing and sweet potato pie, Linda and I went to the movies. We saw the musical, *Black Nativity*, starring Jennifer Hudson, Forest Whitaker, and Angela Bassett. The movie is based on the Langston Hughes gospel play of the same name.

The film tells the story of a troubled family on Christmas Eve. A single mother and her teenage son are being evicted from their Baltimore apartment. The mother sends her son to Harlem to stay with her parents, grandparents the boy has never met. It is a difficult time for everyone. The boy is confused and angry, his mother is wracked with worry and guilt, and his grandparents are clueless as to how to reach out to their estranged daughter and how to deal with this stranger-grandson who wants nothing to do with them. This modern-day story of a family in crisis is set against the backdrop of the nativity story. Yet, somehow, in the midst of all this hurt, there is hope.

I'm not suggesting that God will give us whatever we pray for. But when we place our trust in God and remain faithful to him, there is hope. Elizabeth and Zechariah had a son, and they named him John. There's a line in *Black Nativity* that says, "When a mother bestows a name on her child, it reveals her hopes." John came to prepare the way, but Jesus is the way, and the truth, and the life When we place our faith in him, we always have hope.

Back when the Orioles played at the old Memorial Stadium in Baltimore, I went with some fellows from my church to see a game. I was disappointed because our seats were under an overhang and I did not see any way that a foul ball could ever reach us. I expressed my disappointment to my friends Joel Hawthorne and Bob Hall about where we were sitting. "Darn it," I said (or something to that effect), "we're never going to catch a ball here." Well, the very first inning, Bob Hall caught a foul ball. He was right next to me. I had not counted on the trajectory of the ball coming in under the overhang. I learned a lesson that day about not giving up hope.

I still go to baseball games from time to time—at Camden Yards to see the Orioles, or in southeast Washington to see the Nationals, or even in Bowie to see the Baysox.

I don't have a baseball glove to take to the game anymore. But I always wear a hat, even for night games, just in case a foul ball should come my way.

Never say "never." Live in hope. Trust in God. Do the right thing. Keep believing. God is good. God's love endures. There's no telling what the Lord will do.

ANGELS IN ADVENT
(Luke 1:5-20)

Christmas is full of angels. Read the nativity stories in Matthew and Luke and notice how often angels made an appearance. According to Luke, an angel of the Lord appeared to the priest Zechariah during his service in the Temple. The angel promised that Zechariah and his wife Elizabeth, though aged and beyond childbearing years, would become parents to a son who would be "great in the sight of the Lord." Then in the sixth month of Elizabeth's pregnancy, the same angel Gabriel was sent by God to a village in Galilee to a virgin named Mary, who was engaged to a man named Joseph. Mary was Elizabeth's young cousin, and though of the age to bear a child, she was not yet married to Joseph. Gabriel promised that Mary, like her kinswoman Elizabeth, would bear a special son.

Upon learning of Mary's miraculous pregnancy, Joseph also had a visit from an angel of the Lord—this time in a dream. Joseph had decided to dismiss Mary quietly and call off the wedding, but the angel told Joseph not to be afraid to take Mary as his wife. Then, after Jesus was born in Bethlehem, an angel of the Lord appeared to shepherds who were keeping watch over their flock by night. The angel announced good news of great joy, the birth of a Savior who is the Messiah, the Lord. Suddenly, the angel was joined by a multitude of the heavenly host, praising God and saying, "Glory to God in the highest heaven, and on earth peace among those whom he favors." You hardly can move through the Christmas story without bumping into an angel!

The Greek word for angel means "messenger." Angels of the Lord were God's messengers. In the Christmas story, angels were terrifying (they always had to say, "don't be afraid"), but their messages were good news. Not many people would associate Christmas with fear nowadays. Who's afraid of Christmas? Maybe that's because our Christmases too seldom are touched by an angel.

Our story begins with a priest named Zechariah, who belonged to the priestly division of Abijah. There were 24 divisions of priests in Israel, with each division serving in the Temple in Jerusalem two weeks out of the year. The rest of the time, most of the priests had secular jobs, as farmers, merchants, craftsmen, whatever. Zechariah was married to Elizabeth, who also was descended from a priestly line. Though a priest was permitted to marry any godly woman, marrying a woman of priestly ancestry was considered a special sign of piety. Such righteous people would have expected to be blessed with children, yet this priest and this daughter of priests were childless. In a culture where the family was the primary social unit, and where having children was crucial to perpetuating the family line, a barren woman felt particular anguish and shame. Not only was Elizabeth barren, but she was also past childbearing age. There seemed to be no hope for her and Zechariah.

On this particular day Zechariah had been chosen by lot from among many other priests to burn the incense in the Holy Place of the Temple. This was likely a once-in-a-lifetime honor, probably never to be repeated. This privilege must have been a spiritual highlight in Zechariah's life. But Zechariah got more than he bargained for. An angel of the Lord appeared beside the altar. Zechariah was standing in the Holy Place, as close to God as he could ever hope to be, but he certainly did not expect to see an angel. He was gripped with fear. (It is a common theme in the Bible: just about every time someone sees an angel, they are terrified.) But the angel had good news.

Elizabeth would bear a son, and they would name him John, which means "the Lord has shown favor." Their son would have a special mission to prepare the way for the Messiah. As a sign of his divine calling, John would adopt a vow to abstain from drinking alcohol. Even before his birth, John would be filled with the Holy Spirit. His whole life would be animated by God's presence and power. He would follow in the footsteps of the Old Testament prophet Elijah, whom the Jews believed would return to prepare the way for the Messiah. Even today, Jews leave an empty chair at the table when they celebrate the Passover in the hope that Elijah will return.

The angel's announcement was a lot for Zechariah to comprehend. How could he know that what the angel promised would come true? He was an old man, and his wife was getting on in years, well past the normal childbearing age. The angel replied, "I am Gabriel. I stand in the presence of God and I have been sent to speak to you and to bring you this good news."

Gabriel is one of two angels named in the Old Testament; the other one is Michael. Both Gabriel and Michael are mentioned by name in the book of Daniel. Michael appears in the New Testament in the books of Jude and Revelation. Although Gabriel and Michael are the only two named angels in the Bible, other Jewish and early Christian literature contains the names of other angels. For example, in the book of Tobit in the Apocrypha, Raphael is named as one of the seven holy angels, although Raphael is not mentioned in the Old or New Testaments.

Angels served at God's command to do his will. In the Bible, they deliver God's message, help his people, and punish his enemies. The Bible does not speak of guardian angels, per se, but there is a beautiful passage from the book of Psalms that tells us: "For he will command his angels concerning you to guard you in all your ways. On their hands they will bear you up, so that you will not dash your foot against a stone" (91:11-12).

When Satan sought to tempt Jesus to jump off the pinnacle of the Temple, he quoted Psalm 91 as evidence that God would protect Jesus from falling. When Jesus prayed in agony in the Garden of Gethsemane, an angel from heaven appeared and gave him strength (Luke 22:43). And angels were there at the empty tomb after Jesus had risen from the dead. When Christ returns to earth at the end of time, the trumpet will sound and angels will announce his coming, according to Matthew 24:31 and 1 Thessalonians 4:16. The Bible does not tell us it will be Gabriel who blows the trumpet at the return of Christ, but some traditional songs do. I grew up singing, "The eyes of Texas are upon you, 'til Gabriel blows his horn." If you are not a Texan, you can sing, "O when the saints go marching in, 'til Gabriel blows his horn." Gabriel may or may not be the angel who sounds the last trumpet, but at crucial junctures in the biblical story there are angels.

I don't know about you, but apart from television or the movies, I have never seen an angel—at least not in a form that I could recognize. I have seen people who acted like angels (as well as people who acted like the devil, but that's another story). When my father was nearing the end of his life, the nurses who stayed with him round the clock were pretty close to angels. The same is true of people who work with hospice organizations, or in nursing homes, or on cancer wards, or with AIDS patients, or with severely disabled individuals, or with victims of famine or disasters.

My favorite Christmas movie is the 1946 Frank Capra classic, *It's a Wonderful Life*, starring Jimmy Stewart as George Bailey, a small-town businessman who faces financial ruin due to the incompetence of his uncle and the unscrupulous dirty-dealing of his business rival, Mr. Potter. Seeing no way to save his company or provide for his family, George decides to kill himself by jumping off the town bridge into the icy river, hoping that his death will appear to be an accident and his wife can claim his $15,000 life insurance policy. But just as George is about to jump into oblivion, an Angel Second-Class named Clarence Oddbody hurls himself into the water, confident that George will dive in to save him. After they are both rescued by the bridge operator, Clarence reveals his identity to George.

George is incredulous. Clarence does not look like an angel. He looks like an addled old man, with rumpled clothing and a disheveled shock of white hair. George says, "Well, you look about like the kind of angel I'd get. Sort of a fallen angel, aren't you? What happened to your wings?" Clarence replies, "Well, I haven't earned them yet." But over the course of the rest of the movie, Clarence helps George to see what life would have been like had he never been born. In the end, George comes to his senses and realizes that in spite of his problems, it really is a wonderful life, and Clarence, Angel Second-Class, finally earns his wings.

Clarence looks like the kind of angel most of us would get, because God often sends his messengers in the guise of ordinary people. If you look for wings and halos, you likely will be disappointed. Most angels come incognito. Jesus came that way too. The Word became flesh and dwelt among us. May God use you as his angel to share the Good News.

QUESTIONS FOR DISCUSSION/REFLECTION

1. Have you ever been touched by an angel?
2. Why do bad things happen to good people?
3. Notice that the angel Gabriel appeared to Zechariah during an act of worship. What does this say about the attitude we should have toward worship?
4. Zechariah was speechless after the angel appeared. Is this akin to what Paul was talking about in Romans 8:26, "with sighs too deep for words"?
5. Who are some messengers that God has sent into your life?

NOTE

[1]Lacey Dunkin's story was told by Gail O'Connor in *Parents Magazine*, April 4, 2016; by Rose Minutaglio in *People*, May 4, 2016; and by Rebecca Shinners at WomansDay.com, May 11, 2016.

CHAPTER 6

THE ANNUNCIATION

(Luke 1:26-28)

"Greetings, favored woman! The Lord is with you! … for God has decided to bless you!
You will become pregnant and have a son, and you are to name him Jesus. The Holy
Spirit will come upon you, and the power of the Most High will overshadow you.
So the baby to be born will be holy, and he will be called the Son of God."

(Luke 1:28, 30b, 31, 35 NLT)

Mary was a virgin, engaged to be married to a man named Joseph. Since most young women were expected to marry and have children, there was nothing outwardly unusual about her life. Imagine her shock when the angel Gabriel appeared to her and said, "Greetings, favored one! The Lord is with you." Sensing her confusion, the angel continued: "Do not be afraid, Mary, for you have found favor with God. And now, you will conceive in your womb and bear a son, and you will name him Jesus. He will be great, and will be called the Son of the Most High, and the Lord God will give to him the throne of his ancestor David. He will reign over the house of Jacob forever, and of his kingdom there will be no end."

Naturally, Mary was more than a little perplexed. She asked the angel, "How can this be since I am a virgin?" Unlike today, a woman conceiving a child outside of marriage was a scandal. Mary recognized that becoming pregnant would likely jeopardize her impending marriage to Joseph.

At this point in the story, Mary did not know that an angel would later appear to Joseph in a dream. All she knew was that conceiving a baby before marriage was a huge social taboo. It would disrupt her life forever. Did God really want her to violate the trust that Joseph and her family had placed in her when she was engaged to be married?

The angel explained that no immorality would be involved. "The Holy Spirit will come upon you, and the power of the Most High will overshadow you; therefore the child to be born will be holy; he will be called Son of God." To explain the seemingly impossible, the angel added, "And now, your relative Elizabeth in her old age has also conceived a son, and this is the sixth month for her who was said to be barren. For nothing will be impossible with God."

The crux of the story is that Mary came to peace with a situation she neither expected nor wanted. It was certainly not Mary's plan or desire to become pregnant before marriage. No woman in her day would have wanted that. It certainly was not her goal to give birth to the Son of God. The whole idea must have been overwhelming to her.

Yet, not knowing at the time how Joseph would react to the news, Mary trusted in God. With utter faith she said, "Here am I, the servant of the Lord." Mary made peace with what was being asked of her. It was not what she expected, it was not what she wanted, and she did not understand how it could happen, but she made peace with it. If this is what God wanted of her, then she trusted that God would take care of her.

PROOF OF HEAVEN
(Luke 1:26-35)

It was around five in the morning on November 10, 2008 that Dr. Eben Alexander awoke with intense pain in his head. Alexander, a 54-year-old Harvard-educated neurosurgeon, had trouble speaking, so his wife called 911. When he arrived at the hospital—the same hospital where he regularly performed surgery—the attending physician in the emergency room said that Alexander could utter only one word: "Help!"

Over the next several hours his entire cerebral cortex shut down and he lost all consciousness. The doctors determined that he had contracted a rare and potentially fatal case of E. coli bacterial meningitis. The part of his brain responsible for higher neurological function—consciousness, thought, memory, emotion, understanding—went dark. His doctors gave him little chance to live. Even if he did survive, they said he would probably be brain-damaged for the rest of his life. Nurses would come in and pull back his eyelids and shine a flashlight into his eyes, but there was no response. His wife said, "It was just like no one was there."

After seven days the medical team began weighing the appropriateness of discontinuing treatment. Brain scans showed that Alexander's cortex was not functioning, so they considered taking him off the ventilator. Suddenly, to everyone's utter amazement, Dr. Alexander opened his eyes and started to wake up. Against all odds he regained consciousness, and eventually he made a full recovery. By all accounts it was a medical miracle, but that is only part of the story.

After coming out of the coma, Dr. Alexander began to talk about what he had experienced during those seven days of unconsciousness. Even though there had been no discernible brain function due to the infection, he could remember what he had experienced while comatose. His older son encouraged him to write everything down so that his memories could be preserved. Over the next six weeks he wrote more than 20,000 words describing his experience.

Doctor Alexander wrote that while he had had no body consciousness, he was aware of "a beautiful, spinning white light that had a melody, an incredibly beautiful melody with it that opened up into a bright valley." Next, he was aware of a beautiful woman who soared with him on a butterfly wing. She looked at him and, though she spoke no words, the message came to him: "You are loved; you are cherished; there's nothing you have to fear." Those memories became the basis of his book, *Proof of Heaven: A Neurosurgeon's Journey into the Afterlife.*

Since the book was published there have been plenty of skeptics, especially among his fellow physicians. How could someone with such severe brain damage remember anything while unconscious? Some have tried to explain his account as nothing more than a vivid dream or hallucinations. But Dr. Alexander counters, which is precisely the point: the part of his brain that might dream or have hallucinations was not functioning. As a neurosurgeon who has performed thousands of operations on the brain, he understands how the cerebral cortex works. "I know this [was] not a hallucination, not a dream, not what we call a confabulation. I know that it really occurred, and it occurred outside my brain." Alexander is scientifically certain that his nonfunctioning brain could not have produced what he experienced.

While the infection raged, the sugar level around his brain—normally measuring 60–80, and in a bad case of meningitis down to 20—went down to just 1. He was barely alive. According to Dr. Alexander, "The severity of the meningitis would have prevented dreams, hallucinations, confabulations because those things all require a fairly coordinated amount of cortex"—and his cortex was almost dead. How then does he explain experiencing heaven while he was so deep in unconsciousness? He says that "our consciousness, our soul, our spirit, does not depend on the existence of the brain in the physical universe." In other words, the soul, the spirit, consciousness can exist outside the body.

Now, this is from a man who was not particularly religious before his illness, a man with a scientific mind and a natural skepticism, a physician who before his illness questioned the very idea of a soul or spirit or awareness apart from brain activity. Before he was stricken, Dr. Alexander explained near-death experiences in his patients as simply fantasies produced by brains under extreme stress. Before he spent a week in coma, Dr. Alexander could not reconcile his knowledge of neuroscience with any belief in God or heaven or life beyond the physical world. But after experiencing heaven when his brain was basically dead, Dr. Alexander is a changed man.

He no longer dismisses faith as just wishful thinking. Now, he is convinced that there is a larger reality beyond the physical world and that we can experience that reality even after our brains are no longer functioning. In other words, Dr. Alexander is now convinced there is an afterlife, a reality more real than the physical world we can see and touch and understand. He is confident that his journey into the afterlife provides "proof of heaven."

Our scripture passage is also about an encounter with another world, a reality more real than the physical world we can see and touch and understand. Mary did not see a beautiful woman on a butterfly wing; she saw an angel. Gabriel appeared to Mary with a message that would change her life just as profoundly as Dr. Alexander was changed. Mary would conceive and bear a child who would be the Son of the Most High. "How can this be," she asked, "since I am a virgin?" The angel answered, "The Holy Spirit will come upon you, and the power of the Most High will overshadow you."

The angel's words sound about as improbable as a neurosurgeon lapsing into a coma and taking a journey into the afterlife. Clearly, we are talking about mystery here, beyond this world of time and space, beyond what seems humanly possible. Dr. Alexander says it was scientifically impossible for him to dream or hallucinate about heaven when his cerebral cortex had ceased to function. Mary said it was impossible for a virgin to have a baby, much less the Son of the Most High. Some things seem humanly impossible, but nothing is impossible with God.

Most churches use the four Sundays of Advent to prepare for Christmas. We need four weeks to get ready because Christmas is an encounter with another world. The whole idea of God taking on human flesh and dwelling among us is too big to take in all at once. Christmas means that there is more to reality than what we can see and touch and understand. There is another world, a vastly greater world. Christmas is about that greater reality breaking through into our realm of time and space. This life, this world, is not all there is. A light shines in the darkness, and the darkness can never overcome it.

Doctor Alexander admits even he had a hard time believing that what he had experienced while unconscious was real. But then, sometime after he recovered from the illness, he saw a picture of a woman who he learned was his biological sister. He had never met her, never heard about her, because he was adopted as a small child and he did not know he had a sister. On top of that, his biological sister had died several years earlier, before he ever had the chance to meet her. But when he saw her photograph he was awestruck. He recognized that the woman in the photograph was the same woman who had soared with him beyond time and space on a butterfly wing. At that moment of seeing his departed sister's photo, he knew that his experience in heaven was real. It was not a dream; it was not a hallucination; it was not a confabulation. A beautiful woman he had never known was there in heaven to give him a message that would change his life: You are loved; you are cherished; you have nothing to fear.

No one has ever seen God, but Jesus came to give us a picture of who God is. And Jesus came to give us a message that will change our lives forever: You are loved; you are cherished; you have nothing to fear.

Many churches begin the journey through Advent with Communion. That may seem odd, considering that Christmas is about the birth of Jesus and the Lord's Supper is about his death. But both the beginning and the end of Jesus' life on earth were gifts of love. And now Jesus is with us in Spirit as he continues to bridge the gap between this world and the world to come. Eben Alexander has an amazing story to tell, but the true "proof of heaven" is Jesus. He is our link to the greater reality that transcends time and space and the physical world that is our temporary home. Because of Jesus, we know that we have a permanent home in heaven. Sometimes we catch a glimpse of that future glory, and that gives us just enough hope to live faithfully until the Father calls us home. God took on human flesh and dwelt among us on this terrestrial plain.

NOTHING IS IMPOSSIBLE WITH GOD
(Luke 1:26-38)

When I was a boy, the Christmas portion of Handel's oratorio, *Messiah,* was presented at my home church one Sunday night every December. I probably heard it eight or ten times as I was growing up. At first, I hated it. It was way too long, and the music was too highbrow, and I did not understand a lot of it. As I grew older, I was able to follow the words to the songs, as they were printed in the program, but in some ways that only made matters worse. There was so much repetition. The soloists or the chorus would sing the same words over and over again. I remember thinking to myself, "Why can't they just sing the words once and move on?" You see, I did not understand the purpose of the oratorio. I thought the purpose was to get to the end of it as quickly as possible. But over the years, as I listened to *Messiah* again and again, I began to understand that the purpose was not to get to the end of it as quickly as possible: the repetition was part of the intended experience. The words to the oratorio, taken directly from the Bible, were sung again and again to allow the listeners to hear them again and again, and to reflect on what those words mean.

In a similar way, we read the same scripture passages again and again every year during the Advent season. Chances are, you have heard this scripture passage many times before. God sent the angel Gabriel to a village in Galilee called Nazareth to a young woman named Mary, who was engaged to a man named Joseph. Mary was surprised to be visited by an angel, and even more perplexed when she heard the angel's message. Mary, even though she was not yet married, would have a baby, and not just any baby. Her child would be the Son of God. "How can this be," Mary asked, "since I am a virgin?"

Mary knew the facts of life. She was not yet married, and having a child back then without the benefit of marriage was unthinkable. Young women remained chaste before marriage, so a premarital pregnancy was impossible. But the angel said, "Nothing will be impossible with God. The Holy Spirit will come upon you, and the power of the Most High will overshadow you." Mary replied, "Here I am, the servant of the Lord; let it be according to your word."

We hear this same story year after year, Advent after Advent, Christmas after Christmas. The story is the same, but there is new meaning every time we hear it because we are not the same. Our lives are not in the same place as they were before. And so, we hear the story in a new way. The same familiar words speak a new meaning. What new meaning might this story have for you? Here are some possibilities:

- God comes to us in unexpected times and places.
- God offers us a gift beyond our expectations or deserving.
- God wants to use us to bring blessings to others.
- The Holy Spirit will come upon us, and the power of the Most High will overshadow us if we are willing to be used by God.
- God wants us to be servants of the Lord.

Do you see how rich this story is with possible meaning for our lives? Here is another meaning that has come to me through this story: "Nothing is impossible with God."

In his book, *The Hopeful Heart*, one of my former pastors, John Claypool, told about a conversation he had with a friend who was a rabbi. His rabbi friend said: "To the Jew, there is only one unforgivable sin, and that is the sin of despair. Humanly speaking, despair is presumptuous. It is saying something about the future that we have no right to say, because we have not been there yet and do not know enough." To put it another way, despair is presumptuous, because "nothing is impossible with God." Now, this does not mean that God will do whatever we ask him to do. It does not mean that God will heal every disease, mend every broken relationship, and solve every problem. But as Christians, we remember that Jesus said, "I will never leave you nor forsake you" (Heb. 13:5). And as Christians, we affirm with the apostle Paul that "all things work together for good for those who love God" (Rom. 8:28). All things work together for good, not because everything that happens is good, but because God is good, and God will never leave us or forsake us, and nothing is impossible with God.

Humanly speaking, Mary could not understand how she could have any baby, much less how she could become mother to the Son of God. It seemed impossible, but Mary was beginning to learn that nothing is impossible with God. Beyond all human understanding, Mary would have a baby, and the baby would be the Son of the Most High. Mary's life would be blessed, but that did not mean she would be free from all pain and heartache. The blessings of God do not shield us from the pains of life. But God can use those painful experiences to make us better people. Nothing is impossible with God.

There is a line in the Christmas carol, "It Came Upon the Midnight Clear," that has always touched me. The third verse begins, "And ye, beneath life's crushing load, whose forms are bending low." In the midst of the joy and celebration of the Christmas season, the carol reminds us that life is not always easy. It reminds us that sometimes we can be bent low by crushing loads, even at Christmastime.

Psychiatrist Gordon Livingston wrote a book titled, *Too Soon Old, Too Late Smart: Thirty Things You Need to Know Now.* The book was the outgrowth of Dr. Livingston's painful life experiences, including a tour of duty in Vietnam and the tragic death of two sons within the span of less than a year. His oldest son committed suicide at the age of 22, after a long struggle with bipolar disorder. His youngest son, age six, was diagnosed with leukemia shortly after his brother's death. He died only a few months later, following complications from a bone marrow transplant. Out of those tragic events in his own life, and hearing about the burdens of patients through his psychiatric practice, Dr. Livingston wrote a book about what he learned from life's crushing loads. He said, "The lesson, if there is a lesson to be learned . . . is that we endure what we must." He concluded that life is not fair. Bad things and sad things happen, often to innocent people. Doctor Livingston does not offer any pious platitudes. Sometimes, he says, the best we can do is just survive—just hold on and keep going.

Edmund Sears, author of the words to "It Came Upon the Midnight Clear," was a Unitarian minister in Massachusetts when he wrote the poem in 1849. He was deeply concerned about the recent war that the United States had waged with Mexico, and about the institution of slavery. It may be that Sears was thinking about the slaves when he wrote about those who were bending low beneath life's crushing load. A staunch abolitionist, he had a deep empathy for all people who were hurting, especially the African-American slaves. His hymn was both a subtle protest against slavery and a word of hope for those who were enslaved.

The angel Gabriel came to Mary with a word of hope. She did not understand it at first. The idea that she would have a baby was anything but encouraging news. Having a child out of wedlock was a serious sin. An unmarried mother in that society was a pariah, an outcast. At first hearing, Mary faced the prospect of losing Joseph and her future, and perhaps never having a husband because of social ostracism. But what appeared to be a crushing load was actually an unimagined blessing.

The message of the Christmas story is that no matter how bad things may seem, there is always hope. The crushing loads of life may bend us low, but in every difficult circumstance, God is there. In every burden, every trial, every pain, every heartache, God is there. He who gave a baby to a virgin, he who caused a barren old woman to be with child, is not limited by human limitations. As the angel said, "Nothing is impossible with God." This does not mean that life would be easy, but he promised he would always be with us. Somehow, that is enough.

ANGELS IN ADVENT: MARY
(Luke 1:26-38)

In 2005, I read an article in the *Washington Post* about a teacher in New York who was fired because she was going to have a baby. The problem was not that she was going to have a baby, but that she was not married. The 26-year-old woman taught in a Roman Catholic school, and the conditions of her employment stated that teachers must adhere to Catholic morality. The irony is that if this unwed expectant mother had decided to have an abortion, and had not told anyone about it, she could have kept her job. But by deciding to keep her baby, she lost her job. Of course, teachers are expected to set a good moral example for their students. But doesn't Christian morality also include forgiveness and grace?

If Mary of Nazareth had been a teacher in that Catholic school, she would have been fired. How is that for irony? Mary was not married, and yet she was going to have a baby. Of course, Mary was probably too young to teach in a school. In the first century, Jewish girls typically were engaged to be married between the ages of 12 and 14. The engagement carried the legal status of being married, except that she and her fiancé would not live together until after the marriage ceremony, which was usually about a year after the betrothal. During that engagement period, the woman was expected to remain a virgin. If the woman became pregnant before the wedding ceremony, her infidelity was tantamount to adultery. Her fiancé could call off the wedding and even take her to court and have her publicly humiliated.

Can you imagine Mary's reaction when she was visited by an angel? There she was: a young teenager, engaged (probably arranged by her parents) to a man named Joseph, living in a small agricultural village with a population of no more than a couple thousand people. Her hometown of Nazareth was so insignificant that it was never even mentioned in the Old Testament, or in the writings of the Jewish historian Josephus, or in any other Jewish literature of the time. Mary was probably still living with her parents when the angel Gabriel appeared to her with the words, "Greetings, favored woman! The Lord is with you!"

My guess is that Mary did not feel favored. The angel's news was amazing and troubling at the same time. Mary's mind must have been racing. What will my parents think? What will our neighbors in Nazareth think? What will Joseph think? The promise of a baby is usually a joyous event, except under these circumstances it must have seemed like anything but good news. Yet, Mary said, "I am the Lord's servant, and I am willing to accept whatever he wants."

After my father was diagnosed with an incurable illness, we traveled to Texas to support him and my mother. The doorbell rang Wednesday night around 9:00 p.m. at my parents' home. I answered the door and standing on the front porch was an imposing figure. He was a big guy, with a dark full beard, and with his hair pulled back on his head and hanging down in a ponytail. I noticed he was wearing hospital scrubs and he had a stethoscope around his neck. I surmised he was the nurse coming to cover the night shift for my father. He introduced himself as Jessie, and yes, he had come to stay up all night and take care of my dad.

Later that night, while my father was fitfully sleeping, Jessie told us his story. He had not always been a hospice nurse. He had started his professional life as a roughneck, working in the oil fields of west Texas. But when he lost his job during the oil bust of the late 1980s, Jessie reassessed his life's calling. He went back to school and studied, of all things, nursing. He felt a special calling to work with patients who were dying. After graduating from nursing school, that is what he did. With great kindness and sensitivity and compassion, this former oil field worker poured the oil of comfort on hurting people. He certainly did not look like an angel—no halo, no wings, no angelic glow about him. But he was certainly sent from God to do God's work.

Jessie was not the only angel we met that week. There were Janice and Debra, Venus and Sondra, and Raynelle, the registered nurse who coordinated my father's care. As we got to know them during their 12-hour shifts, we heard the same story over and over again, how each one of them felt called to this work, ministering to the dying and their families. Debra told us it was the most rewarding job she had ever had in nursing. Even the chaplain, Reverend Jim, who had been a pastor for 20 years, said that the past decade of working for the hospice organization were the most fulfilling years of his ministry. How strange that people who work in such difficult situations, with so much pain and grief, should find such satisfaction. Clearly, if they were not called to it, they could not do it. But Jessie and Debra and Jim and all the others felt God had called them into this special and most difficult ministry. Like Mary they answered, "I am the Lord's servant, and I am willing to accept whatever he wants."

Maybe God is not calling you to minister to the dying with a hospice organization, but God does call every Christian into some form of service. I cannot tell you precisely what God wants you to do, but I know that he is calling you to do something in the name of Christ to share his love.

Mary was a young girl when God called her to become the mother of Jesus. She had questions, reservations, and doubts. But in the end, Mary said, "I am the Lord's servant." God is calling you to do something that will make a difference for him. What will your answer be?

QUESTIONS FOR DISCUSSION/REFLECTION

1. Has God ever spoken to you through an "angel"?
2. Mary was confused, disturbed, and had serious questions. Have you ever had questions about what God wanted you to do?
3. Has the Holy Spirit ever come upon you? What were the circumstances?
4. What areas of your life do you see as a calling from God?
5. Can you say, "I am the Lord's servant, and I am willing to accept whatever he wants"?

CHAPTER 7

THE MAGNIFICAT

(Luke 1:39-56)

> *"My soul magnifies the Lord, and my spirit rejoices in God my Savior, for he has looked with favor on the lowliness of his servant."*
>
> (Luke 1:46b-48a NRSV)

The "Magnificat," also known as the "Song of Mary," is a poem/hymn. The title "Magnificat" comes from the first word of the Latin translation. It is based largely on Hannah's song/prayer in 1 Samuel 2:1-10. The phrase "God my Savior" in Luke 1:47 is variously repeated in 1 Timothy 2:3, Titus 3:4, and Jude 25 as "God our Savior." The promise to Abraham in Luke 1:55 comes from Genesis 17:7, 18:18, and 22:17. Following the example of other biblical editors, Luke inserted this psalm into the narrative, as he would do again in 1:68-79 with the "Benedictus" (also from the Latin) of Zechariah. The effect of such poems is to place the events in the larger historical context of God's promises and purposes for his people. The "Magnificat" functions as Mary's response to the declaration by her kinswoman Elizabeth, who was filled with the Holy Spirit: "Blessed are you among women, and blessed is the fruit of your womb" (Luke 1:42).

> *My soul magnifies the Lord,*
> *and my spirit rejoices in God my Savior,*
> *for he has looked with favor on the lowliness of his servant.*
> *Surely, from now on all generations will call me blessed;*
> *for the Mighty One has done great things for me,*
> *and holy is his name.*
> *His mercy is for those who fear him*
> *from generation to generation.*
> *He has shown strength with his arm;*
> *he has scattered the proud in the thoughts of their hearts.*
> *He has brought down the powerful from their thrones,*
> *and lifted up the lowly;*
> *he has filled the hungry with good things,*
> *and sent the rich away empty.*
> *He has helped his servant Israel,*
> *in remembrance of his mercy,*
> *according to the promise he made to our ancestors,*
> *to Abraham and to his descendants forever.* (Luke 1:46-55 NRSV)

THE THINGS THAT MAKE FOR PEACE
(Luke 1:39-56)

The movie *Lincoln* is based on the biography by Doris Kearns Goodwin, *Team of Rivals: The Political Genius of Abraham Lincoln*. The movie covers the last four months of President Lincoln's life. In particular it chronicles his efforts to advance through the House of Representatives the 13th amendment abolishing slavery. Most of the movie takes place in January of 1865. Lincoln had won reelection, and the Civil War was drawing to a close. But the Confederate states were still violently resisting, with casualties on both sides continuing to mount. Lincoln was under intense political pressure to stop the fighting, but he believed that ending the war without ending slavery would be a hollow victory. He had issued the Emancipation Proclamation under his war powers, but once the war was over, Lincoln feared that those slaves he had freed would be enslaved again. Only an amendment to the Constitution, abolishing slavery forever, would lay the foundation for a just and lasting peace.

Just about everyone wanted the war to be over, but not everyone wanted slavery to be over. In Lincoln's own Republican Party many conservatives were not at all sympathetic to the abolitionist cause. Across the aisle, the so-called "Copperhead" Democrats, or "peace" Democrats, wanted to negotiate a peace treaty and restore the Union as it was, with slavery. They were adamantly opposed to the 13th amendment. One of the leading Copperheads described their goal with the slogan, "to maintain the Constitution as it is, and to restore the Union as it was." Some newspaper editors supported the Copperheads and hated Lincoln. Even many of those who supported abolishing slavery considered African Americans an inferior race.

To pass the 13th amendment through the House, Lincoln had to hold his own Republican party together and recruit some Democrats to vote in favor too. He targeted lame-duck legislators who had lost their bids for reelection and would soon be out of their jobs. Lincoln was unwilling to offer direct monetary bribes, but he was willing to offer federal jobs once they left office in exchange for voting for the amendment. Lincoln knew that the country was far from ready to accept full racial equality, so he set his sights on the lesser goal of abolishing slavery. Still, it was a long shot. Some were so anxious for the war to end that they did not care whether slavery ended or not. Once the Confederate States rejoined the Union, the chances of passing the 13th amendment would be even more remote. But Lincoln knew that as long as slavery was tolerated, there could never be genuine peace.

The Old Testament prophecy from Isaiah called the Messiah "the Prince of Peace." When the angels announced Jesus' birth to the shepherds with good news of great joy, they sang "peace on earth, good will toward men." But even though Jesus came to bring peace—peace with God, peace in our hearts, peace among people—we all know that lasting peace is elusive. Our world is still torn by strife.

The setting for our scripture passage is the trip that Mary took to a town in the Judean hill country to visit her relative Elizabeth, after the angel announced to Mary that she would have a baby who would be the Son of the Most High. Exactly why Mary traveled to see Elizabeth, the scriptures do not say. Perhaps she left Nazareth to escape the scandal of her unwed pregnancy. Perhaps she went to see Elizabeth for emotional support, or to learn more about having a baby since Elizabeth also was pregnant.

When Elizabeth heard Mary's greeting, the child in her womb leaped for joy. Elizabeth's yet unborn son would become John the Baptist, who would prepare the way for Mary's yet unborn son, Jesus. So, even in the womb of his mother, the yet unborn John was already preparing the way for Jesus.

Mary responded with a spoken prayer, sometime called "The Magnificat," after the first word of the Latin translation. Mary's prayer seems to be based on the prayer of Hannah in the book of 1 Samuel in the Old Testament. Hannah also was a mother who gave birth to a God-blessed child. In Mary's prayer she thanked God for the favor bestowed upon her. So far, not surprising! But what is surprising is that Mary's prayer then turned downright political. Beginning in Luke 1:51, Mary said: "He has shown strength with his arm; he has scattered the proud in the thoughts of their hearts. He has brought down the powerful from their thrones, and lifted up the lowly; he has filled the hungry with good things, and sent the rich away empty."

It was a very odd prayer for an expectant mother to pray: "he has scattered the proud … he has brought down the powerful … and lifted up the lowly." Mary understood that the birth of her son would change the world; that the coming of Jesus would bring about a whole new understanding of the way God wants us to live. Before Jesus, the world lived by the power of the sword: Might made right. The proud and the powerful prevailed over the weak and the lowly. Most people lived basically only for themselves.

Among the Jews there was the tradition of showing compassion to widows and orphans, sojourners and strangers, the weak and the vulnerable. So, some people did care about more than themselves. But even the Jews did not challenge many of the injustices of their time. It took the followers of Jesus to do that. Many of the abolitionists who finally prevailed in abolishing slavery were inspired by their understanding of the teachings of Jesus and the way God wants us to live.

There is much speculation about the religious faith of Abraham Lincoln. He was never baptized, and he never joined a particular church. Part of that is because Lincoln's parents were Baptists, and Baptists do not baptize babies. So, Abraham Lincoln was not baptized as an infant. But he was exposed to Christian beliefs at an early age, and Lincoln largely taught himself to read by reading the Bible. Of all U.S. presidents, perhaps the only one with a greater familiarity with the scriptures than Abraham Lincoln was Jimmy Carter. Lincoln's most famous speeches were laced with biblical imagery. According to historian Bruce Gourley, Lincoln developed his abolitionist views, in part, due to being raised in an anti-slavery Baptist church. Lincoln knew that there could be no peace without justice, and justice meant freeing the slaves and abolishing slavery forever.

When my wife Linda and I saw *Lincoln* in the theater, we noticed that there was a couple sitting a few rows in front of us who left in the middle of the movie. They had come in carrying tubs of popcorn and soft drinks, but about an hour and a half into the film they left and did not come back. I don't know if it was because they had something else to do, or because the popcorn and the soda were gone, or maybe because they just lost interest in the movie. I'll admit, after the battle scene near the beginning, there wasn't a whole lot of exciting action in the film. Most of it was dialogue, and I suppose that couple might have gotten bored by all the talking. But peace was won not by battle alone.

Peace was won by talking that led to abolishing slavery and establishing justice. As the hymn "Lead On, O King Eternal" says: "For not with swords' loud clashing, nor roll of stirring drums, with deeds of love and mercy, the heavenly kingdom comes."

Apollo 8 was the first manned mission to the moon. The astronauts did not actually set foot on the moon, but they circled the moon in their spacecraft some 10 times before returning home. It was the first time that any human had seen the moon up close or seen the whole earth from outer space. Before, astronauts in orbit could only see part of our planet. But on the *Apollo 8* spacecraft astronauts Borman, Lovell, and Anders escaped the earth's gravitational pull and flew all the way into lunar orbit. The flight took place in December of 1968.

Some people had asked NASA to postpone the mission because it would take place over Christmas, and should there be a disaster, that would put a damper on holiday celebrations. But as *Apollo 8* circled the moon on Christmas Eve, there was extra rejoicing here on earth. It is estimated that at least a billion people, a fourth of the world's population at the time, were watching on television. During the third lunar orbit—more than 200,000 miles from home, on Christmas Eve—as the capsule emerged from the back side of the moon yet again and the astronauts could see the whole earth yet again, Commander Frank Borman read a prayer. He said it was a message for the people of his home church in Texas, and "actually to people everywhere." This is what he said:

> Give us, O God, the vision that can see thy love in the world in spite of human failure. Give us the faith to trust thy goodness in spite of our ignorance and weakness. Give us the knowledge that we may continue to pray with understanding hearts. And show us what each one of us can do to set forward the coming of the day of universal peace. Amen.

On the ninth revolution around the moon the three astronauts read the story of Creation in the first 10 verses of the book of Genesis. They closed with these words: "Good night, good luck, a Merry Christmas and God bless all of you—all of you on the good earth." Commander Borman later said, "I thought then, and I continue to think now, the voyage of *Apollo 8* was really the final leg in my own personal religious experience... We were closer to [the moon] than any man had ever been before—really only 60 miles away—and we were drawn to the moon. [But as we] looked back ... our thoughts were drawn to Earth... Everything that we held dear was back on Earth. I was just struck by the sensation that there was an almighty hand that created that beautiful place."

From their vantage point in orbit around the moon, the three astronauts of *Apollo 8* could see the earth—the whole earth, the good earth. They wanted to say something to signify one world, something to summon everyone on the earth to learn to live together in peace. They saw that the moon was a cold, barren, and inhospitable place. But the earth was home, and our home too. We must learn to get along with one another. We must, each one of us, do something "to set forward the coming of the day of universal peace." Jesus said, "Blessed are the peacemakers, for they will be called children of God" (Matt. 5:10). Peace with God, peace in our hearts, peace with each other—Jesus came to give us peace. Lord may it be.

CLEAR AS MIDNIGHT
(Luke 1:39-56)

The year was 1849. New England was awakening to the Industrial Revolution. The town of Wayland, Massachusetts, once a sleepy little village of farmers and merchants, was becoming an urban center. A small shop to manufacture shoes had opened two decades before, and within another two decades Wayland would be home to nine shoe factories, employing more than 500 workers. Farmers and their families were leaving the country-side and moving into town to work in the mills and factories. The social upheaval caused by the Industrial Revolution meant that tens of thousands would leave their agrarian way of life for cramped urban dwellings and long hours of tedious, relentless labor. To add to the turmoil, a civil war was brewing. Tensions between abolitionists and slaveholders were pushing the North and the South to inevitable conflict.

By this time, Wayland was home to the radical abolitionist editor and writer, Lydia Maria Child, who was outspoken in her condemnation of slavery. The pastor of the Unitarian church in Wayland was Edmund H. Sears, an independent thinker who believed and preached the divinity of Christ. It was during this time of social unrest that Rev. Sears wrote a poem that became one of our most beloved Christmas carols, "It Came Upon the Midnight Clear." The tenor of those troubled times was reflected in the words of the poem, especially in verse 3:

Yet with the woes of sin and strife
The world has suffered long;
Beneath the angel-strain have rolled
Two thousand years of wrong;
And man, at war with man, hears not
The love-song which they bring;
O hush the noise, ye men of strife,
And hear the angels sing.

This stanza could have been written today, could it not?

Our scripture passage is sometimes called, "The Magnificat," taken from the first word in the Latin translation of Mary's song. It's the song that Mary sang about the coming birth of her son. It seems a strange song for an expectant mother to sing, but it begins reasonably enough in *The Message* translation:

I'm bursting with God-news;
I'm dancing the song of my Savior God.
God took one good look at me, and look what happened—
I'm the most fortunate woman on earth!
What God has done for me will never be forgotten,
the God whose very name is holy, set apart from all others.

Mary was excited, as any first-time mother would be. She praised God for the gift of the precious baby that would be born to her. The first part of her song is what we would expect from a young woman expecting a baby. But the second part of Mary's song is not what we would expect: it speaks of profound social changes and political upheaval.

> His mercy flows in wave after wave
>   on those who are in awe before him.
> He bared his arm and showed his strength,
>   scattered the bluffing braggarts,
> He knocked tyrants off their high horses,
>   pulled victims out of the mud.
> The starving poor sat down to a banquet;
>   the callous rich were left out in the cold.

Not exactly a mother's lullaby, is it? Mary foresaw that the coming of Jesus would have profound consequences for the social order. William Temple was Archbishop of Canterbury in the early 1940s during the Second World War, while India was still a colony of the United Kingdom. Because the people of India were longing for independence from Great Britain, Archbishop Temple cautioned the Anglican missionaries in India not to read the Magnificat in public. He feared that if the Indian people heard it, it might be so inflammatory as to start a revolution.

Jesus came to change the world. The 19th-century abolitionists, such as Lydia Maria Child, understood that. They understood that the birth of Jesus was more than a quaint, picturesque story. They understood that Jesus came to set the captives free. So, inspired by the message of Jesus, they agitated to change the social order, even at the cost of a terrible civil war. Edmund Sears understood the changes that Jesus came to bring. He saw that the Industrial Revolution meant the overthrow of the agrarian way of life for thousands of people, for whom midnight was still upon the earth. Sears and other social reformers were concerned about the upheaval wreaked by the urbanization and industrialization of society, and they sought to create a more humane culture based on justice and compassion, rather than materialism and greed. Bishop William Temple understood the revolutionary message of the song of Mary for the people of India.

So, the first message of Mary's song is this: You cannot celebrate the coming of the Christ child and be content with the world the way it is. As long as there is hunger and poverty, as long as there is oppression and injustice, as long as man is at war with man, as long as innocent children are the victims of strife, we cannot hear the angels sing. Jesus came to set things right in the world. Jesus came to awaken the consciences of his followers to the sufferings and the injustices of downtrodden people, and to do something about it. Jesus came not to leave the world as it was, but to change the social order. Mary understood that and sang about it in her song.

There is a second truth here that Mary understood. Jesus came not only to change the social order, but also to change the hearts of people. And the way that God changes our hearts is to embrace us with his love. In her song Mary said: "He embraced his chosen child, Israel; He remembered and piled on the mercies, piled them high." The third stanza of Edmund Sears' hymn speaks to our human condition, both the social ills of the day and the individual, personal burdens we all bear:

> And ye, beneath life's crushing load,
> Whose forms are bending low,
> Who toil along the climbing way
> With painful steps and slow,
> Look now! for glad and golden hours
> come swiftly on the wing.
> O rest beside the weary road,
> And hear the angels sing!

Christmas is about the mercies of God, piled on high. It is about God bending low to lift us up when we are stooped beneath life's crushing load. It is about God coming alongside to walk with us when we toil with slow and painful steps along life's path. Christmas is about resting beside the weary road, and hearing the angels sing.

In the short story, "Clear as Midnight," by Alicia McKenzie, Nathan Summers is devastated by the death of his father. The story opens with Nathan kneeling in the snow beside his father's grave and laying a rose on top of the stone marker. Nathan knows his father cannot hear him, but he finds himself having a one-way conversation with a chunk of marble. "I miss you," Nathan whispers, an admission he had not intended to make. Unwilling to allow himself to weep, Nathan gets up, turns around, and heads back toward the house through the snow.

Nathan can hear Christmas music playing before he reaches the back door, but he does not feel like celebrating. In fact, he would prefer to remain outside by himself, except that he knows his wife Jean will be expecting him to rejoin the family. So, Nathan knocks the snow off his boots and goes inside. He walks down the hallway into the den. The room is empty. Nathan pours himself a glass of eggnog.

"Where is everybody?" Nathan asks as Jean passes by.

"Wrapping presents," Jean replies. "Drink your eggnog and get warm, Nate. You were out in the snow a long time."

"I like the snow," Nathan comments.

"Did you change your mind about going to church?" Jean wonders.

"Ask me in an hour," Nathan answers.

Almost offhandedly Jean says, "Oh, something came for you today. I put it under the tree."

Nathan goes over to the tree to investigate. It is a small, square package. His name is written on the front in print he does not recognize. Nathan takes a seat in the chair next to the window and begins to open the package. Inside he finds a flat, glossy black box. He lifts the top carefully. His heart rate jumps as he opens the card containing handwriting he does recognize. It is from his mother, recently widowed. He swallows hard and reads:

Yet with the woes of sin and strife
The world has suffered long;
Beneath the angel-strain have rolled
Two thousand years of wrong;
And man, at war with man, hears not
The love-song which they bring;
O hush the noise, ye men of strife,
And hear the angels sing.

The lump in Nathan's throat grows larger. He wonders what his mother is trying to tell him. The words are from a Christmas carol, aren't they? Turning the card over, he sees another verse on the back:

For lo! The days are hastening on by prophet bards foretold
When with the ever-circling years come round the age of gold
When peace shall over all the earth its ancient splendors fling
And the whole world give back the song which now the angels sing.

Nathan takes a deep sigh and closes his eyes. He can see what his mother is trying to tell him, but he isn't sure whether he is ready to hear her yet—whether he can believe that all of this has a purpose, that there is something brighter at the end of it. He sets down the card and opens the box. It is a silver pocket watch. From the color of the silver and the weight of the timepiece, it has to be at least a hundred years old. Watches like this one aren't made anymore. On the back he spies a tiny set of initials and a date: "1880." He opens the case to see the face. Roman numerals, with delicate, fragile-looking hands—yet the watch is working. The hands are moving, just as they have for 120 years.

Looking at the watch, Nathan begins to understand what his mother had meant by sending it to him. Life goes on, time goes on. And there is nothing he can do to recapture the hours and days and months and years that have passed by. He must not let the future slip through his fingers while he mourns the past. Nathan's eyes blur. He feels raw—exposed, as if he is back out in the snow at his father's grave. The tears come, and he lets them fall. He can count on one hand the number of times since he was 13 years old that he has let himself cry. He watches the falling snow through his tears, and something eases inside him. The pain does not go away, but it eases.

"Nathan," Jean calls, "I was just wondering if you were coming with us to the Christmas service."

Nathan thinks for a moment and then calls back, "I think I will." Then he grins and looks down at the watch. He has just enough time to wrap Jean's present before they have to leave.

Jesus came to change the world, and to change our hearts. He came to give us rest beside the weary road of life, and respite from life's crushing load. The snow still falls; sometimes the tears fall too. But the pain is eased, and somehow the burdens of life are changed to joy. Come, hush the noise, you people of strife, and hear the angels sing.

HOLY IS HIS NAME
(Luke 1:46-49)

There is something about Mary that causes us ambivalence. Protestants in general have an uneasy relationship with Mary. We respect her and admire her as the mother of Jesus, but we are reluctant to elevate her to the lofty status that the Catholic Church has done. To Catholics she is the Blessed Virgin, just a little lower than Jesus himself. Many Roman Catholics pray to Mary, or claim to have seen visions of the Blessed Virgin, or ascribe miracles to her intervention. Many such beliefs about Mary go far beyond what can be found in scripture, for example:

- In the 8th century, a theologian named Germanus of Constantinople claimed that Mary dispenses graces to the church on Earth.
- In the 8th century, Mary was given the title "Mediatrix," meaning that Mary shares in the saving mission of her son, mediating God's grace.
- In the 12th century, Bernard of Clairvaux popularized the teaching that Mary dispenses grace to Christians.
- In the 12th century, the "Hail Mary" prayer was used in conjunction with praying the Rosary.
- By the 13th century, cathedrals were dedicated to Mary, and the veneration of Mary became even more pronounced.
- Late in the 14th century, Mary was called the "Coredemptrix," meaning that she was involved in the redeeming work of her son.
- In the 16th century, the Council of Trent defended the idea that Mary and the saints can intercede for Christians.
- Into the 19th and 20th centuries, shrines to Mary appeared at Lourdes and Fatima and other places, and miracles were claimed to have taken place through her intervention.

The Protestant Reformation in the 16th century was deeply suspicious of many of the practices of the Roman Catholic Church that were not based on scripture. Martin Luther and the other Reformers respected Mary as the humble, obedient mother of our Lord, but they rejected praying to Mary or to any other saint for divine assistance or intervention. The Reformers also rejected teachings about Mary that they considered legendary, such as the "immaculate conception," the idea that from the moment of her conception Mary was preserved from the stain of original sin, or the idea that she remained a perpetual virgin even after she was married, or that Mary's body was assumed into heaven after she died. How all those legends and teachings developed over the centuries is a story in itself. The result for many Protestants is that we are not quite sure what to do about Mary. It is one thing to hear "Ave Maria" sung in church or at a wedding, but quite another to address Mary in prayer.[1]

The biblical references to Mary are surprisingly limited. She appears in Luke 1–2 in the nativity story, followed by presenting the infant Jesus at the Temple, and again taking Jesus to the Temple when he was 12. In John's gospel, Mary asks Jesus to help with the wine at a wedding in Cana, then she appears at the foot of the cross. There is a parallel account in Matthew, Mark, and Luke when Mary visits Jesus with his brothers during his public ministry. And in Acts, Mary is present on the Day of Pentecost when the followers of Jesus receive the Holy Spirit. Other than those relatively few references, Mary is not a major figure in the gospel story. But her subsequent role in the traditions of the church has grown far beyond her role in scripture.

The scripture passage often called "The Magnificat" is Mary's song of praise to God in response to being blessed with the gift of God's Son. "Magnificat" is the first word in the Latin translation of Mary's song, which many English versions translate as "magnifies." "My soul magnifies the Lord, and my spirit rejoices in God my Savior," Mary sang. Notice that the focus of Mary's song was on God, not on herself. Mary saw herself not as something special, but as a humble handmaid of the Lord; not as a subject of veneration, but simply as a recipient of God's love and grace. Future generations would call Mary blessed, not because of what she had done, but because of what God would do through her.

It is difficult to appreciate who Mary was because 20 centuries of Christian devotion and iconography and art have given us an idealized picture of her. In reality, she was a humble figure. Based on the few references in Luke, we can deduce that Mary was a teenage peasant girl from the small town of Nazareth in Galilee, probably with little formal education, and almost certainly from a poor working-class family. Mary had every right to feel humble because she came from a modest and humble background. Other than the fact that she was engaged to Joseph, there was little about Mary to set her apart from the other peasant girls in her village.

Some years ago, my wife Linda participated in a mission trip to Kenya sponsored by Buckner Orphan Care International. The group went to provide a Bible camp experience for children at an orphanage there. Dana Jones, an administrative assistant at the Buckner headquarters in Dallas, kept family members in the U.S. informed about the group's progress in Kenya with emails during the mission trip. In one email Dana wrote:

> I spoke to the group this morning. All were having a great time. The team is working well together, and the Lord is using each of their talents in mighty ways. They decorated Christmas stockings last night, put on a morning VBS, and were at the water park with the kids. The team leader asked one of the little girls if she had slept well. The little girl replied no; she was so excited about the camp that she could not sleep.

I could only imagine the impact that the mission team members had on those orphan children in Kenya. That week at camp must have been one of the most meaningful times of their young lives. To have Christians come all the way from America just to be with them, to teach them, to spend time with them, to share with them, to get to know them, to love them—no wonder that little orphan girl could not sleep. What an amazing blessing to know that someone cares!

In a sense, we are not so far removed from those humble orphan children in Kenya, for the greatest longing of our hearts is to know that someone cares. God sent his Son Jesus to tell us that we have a Father in heaven, and to welcome us into his family. Jesus came all the way from God, just to be with us, to teach us, to spend time with us, to share with us, to get to know us, to love us.

Mary understood the significance of what God had done. She understood how blessed she was, and the gratitude of her humble heart burst forth in song. When we think about it, we must confess that we are not that special ourselves. We are not that deserving of God's favor and grace. But God loves us even in our lowliness. And God came in the person of his Son to pour his love into our humble hearts. And so, each of us has a Magnificat to sing, for we too are blessed. God gave his Son not just to Mary, but to all of us. Like Mary, how can we keep from singing, because of what the Lord has done for us?

QUESTIONS FOR DISCUSSION/REFLECTION

1, Why do you think God chose Mary to be the mother of Jesus?
2. What are the social consequences of the coming of Jesus?
3. What is it about the birth of Jesus that can only be expressed in song?
4. What is your favorite Christmas carol, and why?
5. In what ways has God blessed you with the gift of his Son?

NOTE

[1]Much of the information about the Roman Catholic and Reformers' treatment of Mary Is taken from *Christian History & Biography*, Summer 2004.

CHAPTER 8

THE BIRTH OF JESUS
(Luke 2:1-7)

> *[Joseph] went to be registered with Mary, to whom he was engaged and who was expecting a child. While they were there, the time came for her to deliver her child. And she gave birth to her firstborn son and wrapped him in bands of cloth, and laid him in a manger, because there was no place for them in the inn.*
>
> (Luke 2:5-7 NRSV)

"There was no place for them in the inn." Why? Was the inn full? Did they fail to make a reservation? Did they not have enough money? Were people from Galilee discriminated against when it came to lodging? Did the innkeeper "reserve the right to refuse service to anyone"?

Laying the newborn baby in a manger implies that Joseph and Mary found refuge in a stable. So, Jesus was born in a stable, or maybe in a cave used as a shelter for animals. Mary wrapped the baby in bands of cloth. With no crib for a bed, she laid him in a manger. I suspect that Mary and Joseph were anxious when it was time for Jesus to be born and they had no place to stay. We don't know exactly how they ended up in the stable, but they were okay. They made do. "Away in a manger, no crib for a bed, the little Lord Jesus lay down his sweet head." It was an unconventional place for Jesus to be born, but then again, his whole life would be unconventional.

PERSON OF THE YEAR
(Luke 2:1-7)

I wonder if you can identify some famous people. Harlow Curtice (1893–1962) served as president of General Motors from 1953–1958. In 1955, General Motors sold more than five million vehicles and became the first corporation in American history to earn more than $1 billion in a single year. David Ho (b. 1952) is a Taiwanese-American scientist who is famous for his work in AIDS research. A professor at Columbia University College of Physicians and Surgeons, he heads an AIDS research center. Andrew Grove (1936–2016), a Hungarian-born American scientist, was a pioneer in the semiconductor industry. In the mid-1990s he was the CEO of Intel Corporation, which became the largest semiconductor manufacturer in the world. He was widely considered one of the greatest business leaders of the 20th century.

While you might not recognize the names of Harlow Curtice or David Ho or Andrew Grove, you probably recognize the name of the fourth famous person: Pope Francis, head of the Roman Catholic Church. All four of these men have something in common: They were named *Time* magazine's "Person of the Year" (or what used to be called "Man of the Year"): Harlow Curtice in 1955, David Ho in 1996, Andrew Grove in 1997, and Pope Francis in 2013. All were recognized for the impact they have had on their time.

Time magazine started selecting a Man of the Year back in 1927. Some people think *Time* came up with this designation to make up for an embarrassing omission. The week after aviator Charles Lindbergh made his historic flight across the Atlantic, *Time* failed to put his picture on the cover. To remedy such an egregious editorial error, *Time* made Lindbergh its first Man of the Year with a cover story at the end of 1927. And every year since then, *Time* has had a Person of the Year cover story.

Every U.S. president since 1927 has been named Person of the Year except for Calvin Coolidge, Herbert Hoover, and Gerald Ford. It is usually considered an honor to be named Person of the Year, except not every designee has been particularly honorable, including controversial figures such as Adolf Hitler, Joseph Stalin, Nikita Khrushchev, and Ayatollah Khomeini. After Khomeini was named Person of the Year in 1979, there was such a public outcry that *Time* began to shy away from selecting such polarizing figures. So, for example, in 2001 following the attacks on 9/11, *Time* named Rudolph Giuliani, then the mayor of New York City, as Person of the Year, rather than the figure responsible for the attacks and who had the larger impact on world affairs, Osama bin Laden.

In 2013, *Time* selected Pope Francis as its Person of the Year. The runner-up was Edward Snowden, the government contractor who leaked classified NSA documents to the press, and who is still a fugitive from justice, granted sanctuary in Russia. My guess is that most Americans much preferred to see Pope Francis on the cover of *Time* magazine rather than Edward Snowden. Pope Francis has certainly had a big impact on the Catholic Church and the world in general during his tenure in office.

What makes Pope Francis so notable is as much his style as anything he has done. The pope is a man of the people, a humble figure with a common touch. He seems to eschew the pomp and circumstance of previous popes and instead to project a simpler lifestyle. When Pope Francis was the archbishop of Buenos Aires, he rode public transportation rather than in a chauffeured limosine. He lived in a modest apartment rather than an ecclesiastical palace. When he became pope, Francis brought that unpretentious manner to Rome. There are photos circulating on the Internet comparing him with his predecessor, Pope Benedict. The previous pope is pictured sitting on a gold throne and wearing a gold-embroidered, fur-trimmed stole. Red Prada shoes peak out from beneath his immaculate cassock. He has a gold ring on his finger and a diamond-and-ruby-encrusted cross hanging around his neck. He looks like a medieval monarch. In the companion photo Pope Francis is sitting on a simple wooden chair and wearing black pants and black shoes. The ring on his finger is silver, and the cross around his neck is made of iron. But the differences between the current pope and the previous pope are more than cosmetic.

Pope Francis has become a champion of the poor. He preaches mercy, compassion, and forgiveness. When asked about gay people he responded, "Who am I to judge?"

He has even advocated civil unions for persons of the same sex. In a letter to the Church, he instructed leaders to focus on helping the poor and mending the broken. He's not just talk. Pope Francis washed the feet of female prison inmates. He embraced and kissed a disfigured man whom others would have hesitated to touch. Pope Francis wrote, "I prefer a Church which is bruised, hurting, and dirty because it has been out on the streets, rather than a Church which is unhealthy from being confined and from clinging to its own security."[1]

Washington Post columnist Petula Dvorak noted the irony of Pope Francis being named *Time*'s Person of the Year. First, she said, it was an honor the pope did not seek. Second, the pope was celebrated for simply doing his job. After all, isn't the pope supposed to be like Jesus? Isn't he supposed to preach compassion, model humility, and live a life of service? Dvorak said that it is a sad commentary on our time that a holy man is named Person of the Year just for acting like a holy man. She added that the pope is seen as something extraordinary because "we live in a culture that has largely accepted greed and bad behavior as the norm."[2] By showing humility and compassion and forgiveness and love, Pope Francis is simply doing what all Christians are supposed to do—namely, act like Jesus.

The nativity story in Luke's gospel is so familiar to us that we might easily miss the radical message Luke is trying to convey. The idea of a newborn baby lying in a manger because there was no room for his parents in the inn does not shock us at all, as we've sanitized and domesticated the story. We can't smell the manure of the barnyard nor feel the chill of the night air. We can't identify with the panic Mary and Joseph must have felt. When the time had come for Mary to deliver, they were far from home, afraid and alone. They could not find a decent place for Jesus to be born.

No, the baby in the manger does not shock us because we've turned this story into porcelain crèches and scenes fit for Hallmark greeting cards. But the reality is that Jesus was born into a family so poor, they were basically homeless. His humble birth set the tone for his entire life. The adult Jesus would say, "Foxes have holes and birds of the air have nests, but the Son of Man has nowhere to lay his head" (Matt. 8:20). And the adult Jesus would show extraordinary compassion for the poor, the downtrodden, the power-less, the neglected and rejected and forgotten, the nobodies for whom no one else cared.

The King of Kings and Lord of Lords was born not in a palace in Jerusalem but in a back alley in Bethlehem. His humble birth was a precursor of his humble life. As Mary sang in the Magnificat, he would bring "down the powerful from their thrones" and lift up the lowly. Jesus came not to bless the inequities and injustices of the status quo, but to inaugurate a new kingdom of justice and compassion and love.

One of my heroes is the late preacher/theologian Howard Thurman, who served as dean of the chapel at Howard University, then founded the first interracial church in America in San Francisco, and later served as dean of the chapel at Boston University. Thurman came from a very humble background. Born in 1899, he was raised in Daytona, Florida, in large part by his grandmother who had been a slave. Growing up in the segregated South, Thurman lacked opportunities to continue his education because public schools for African-American children in Daytona only went through the seventh grade. His grandmother scraped together enough money to send him to high school in

Jacksonville, Florida, but Howard used all the money she had given him just to buy his train ticket to Jacksonville.

After buying his ticket he was told that he would have to pay extra to ship his trunk on the train. Literally penniless, young Howard sat down on the steps of the train station and began to cry. A stranger, seeing his distress, paid the charges to send the boy's baggage. The stranger, a black man in overalls, never introduced himself, and Howard never learned his name. But 65 years later, Howard Thurman dedicated his autobiography to "the stranger in the railroad station in Daytona Beach who restored my broken dream."

After college Howard Thurman attended and graduated from Colgate-Rochester Divinity School, a seminary affiliated with American Baptists. In 1936 he led a delegation of African Americans to meet the great reformer from India, Mohandas Gandhi. It was Gandhi who challenged Thurman to rethink the place of Christianity in the social order of segregated America. Up until that time the Christian religion was often used by whites to keep blacks "in their place." But just as Gandhi had advocated nonviolent protest to challenge British colonial rule in India, he asked Thurman if Christianity might have similar power to overcome racism in America.

In 1949 Thurman wrote his seminal book, *Jesus and the Disinherited*, in which he articulated an interpretation of the message and ministry of Jesus that laid the foundation for the Civil Rights Movement. While at Boston University, Thurman became a mentor to a graduate student, Martin Luther King Jr. It was Thurman who introduced King to the idea of Jesus as liberator of the oppressed and to the idea of nonviolent resistance to injustice.

In 2013 Frank Wolf, a Republican congressman from northern Virginia, announced that he would not seek reelection after 30-plus years in Congress. His retirement announcement came as a surprise because Wolf was widely respected, and leaders in both parties expected him to run for an 18th term. But Wolf said he was going to give up his seat in Congress so he could focus on humanitarian issues. He said, "As a follower of Jesus, I am called to work for justice and reconciliation, and to speak for those who cannot speak for themselves."[3]

As a follower of Jesus, Frank Wolf saw a higher calling than serving in the United States House of Representatives. Some might see it as downward mobility to willingly give up power, but isn't that what Jesus did? In Philippians 2:6-8 Paul wrote that Jesus, "who, though he was in the form of God, did not regard equality with God as something to be exploited, but emptied himself, taking the form of a slave, being born in human likeness. And being found in human form, he humbled himself and became obedient to the point of death—even death on a cross." We must never forget that the baby in the manger became the man on the cross. Kind of puts Christmas in perspective, doesn't it? Christmas is more than gifts under the tree; it is the gift of the baby in the manger who became the man on the cross.

Time magazine named Pope Francis as Person of the Year, primarily because the pope is seeking to do what every Christian should seek to do: live like Jesus. That's what God wants from us for Christmas: the gift of ourselves, dedicated to him.

NO PLACE FOR THEM
(Luke 2:1-7)

Alberta Kirkpatrick thought no one wanted her. She thought she had no place in this world. Her mother had died when she was young, and her alcoholic father couldn't take care of her. Her three siblings were scattered elsewhere, and Alberta had been placed with an abusive foster family. She didn't think anyone loved her—or would ever love her. Alberta thought about killing herself. Then, at the age of 11, her life took a dramatic turn. She was taken to the Canterbury Shaker Village in Hanover, New Hampshire. The year was 1929. Alberta Kirkpatrick would become the last child officially reared by that dwindling, celibate community.

Linda and I heard Alberta's story when we visited the Canterbury Shaker Village in New Hampshire. The Village is now a vast indoor and outdoor museum, comprised of 29 restored buildings situated on almost 700 acres of property. In the 19th century, Canterbury was a thriving community of some 300 Shaker brothers and sisters, along with the orphans the Shakers took in to raise. Because the Shakers practiced celibacy, they had no children of their own, except for those families who joined after having children. But the community functioned as a kind of orphanage. The Shakers kept the movement going by attracting new converts and by providing a place for children in need of a home. But in the 20th century the Shaker movement began to die out as fewer and fewer people were interested in a communal, celibate lifestyle, and as society developed alternatives for orphans. The Canterbury Shaker Village became a museum after the last Shaker sister died in 1992.

When Linda and I visited the Canterbury Village we watched a video of Alberta Kirkpatrick describing how she came to live with the Shaker sisters more than 90 years ago. She joined seven other girls whom the Shakers were caring for at the time. In the seven years that she lived there, until age 18, Alberta says she never lacked for food or affection. Alberta said, "They made a living through the Depression for all of us. I'm grateful for the education I got there." Alberta, who lived in Pennsylvania as an adult, returned to Canterbury to celebrate her 90th birthday. The museum held a birthday party for her and invited the townspeople to come and join in the celebration. Alberta was given a birthday cake and lots of attention. She commented: "It was marvelous. It was marvelous. When I was little, I wasn't wanted at all. Now that I'm older, I get this adulation. I can't see that I'm that spectacular of a person, but I certainly loved it all."

In our scripture passage, Mary and Joseph must have known what it felt like to not be wanted. Mary, in particular, must have felt almost all alone in the world. Other than Joseph, she had no one—except the baby she was carrying, and God. Can you imagine the loneliness Mary must have felt? Before they were married, before Joseph understood that the child within her was from the Holy Spirit, he had resolved to break off their engagement quietly, so as not to expose her to public shame. Only after Joseph was told in a dream that Mary had not been unfaithful to him did he change his mind and take her as his wife.

But soon her condition must have become apparent to everyone in the village. Mary must have felt like an outcast for her assumed immorality. How else do you explain Mary traveling with Joseph 80 miles from Nazareth to Bethlehem when the time for to give birth was so near? My guess is that Mary went with Joseph to Bethlehem because she was no longer welcome in Nazareth. Everyone assumed that her pregnancy was a moral failure. Even Joseph assumed that, before the angel told him otherwise in a dream. My guess is that Mary was shunned by her fellow villagers and ostracized by her own family. So, the child within her was conceived by the Holy Spirit? Yeah, right!

You see, the law did not require Mary to travel to Bethlehem with Joseph for the census. Only the man was obligated to register, not his wife. Under normal circumstances, it would have made more sense for Mary to remain behind with family, since the date of her delivery was so close. But these were not normal circumstances. It may be that neither her family nor Joseph's family believed that unbelievable story of how she had become with child. It may be that there was no place for Mary to stay in Nazareth, given her scandalous condition. So, she traveled with Joseph to Bethlehem, 80 miles on foot, or on the back of a donkey, even though her child could come at any time.

No one seemed to want Mary. Other than by Joseph's side, Mary must have felt she had no place in the world. But it got even worse when they arrived in Bethlehem. No one wanted Mary and Joseph there either. Most of our English translations of the Bible say that the newborn Jesus was laid in a manger "because there was no place for them in the inn." Some scholars have interpreted this to mean that Jesus was born in a stable because Joseph and Mary were too poor to afford proper accommodations. That may be so because people with money can almost always find a place to stay. But there is another intriguing possible explanation.

The Greek word that Luke used in chapter 2 that is often translated "inn" is *kataluma*. Technically, this word means not "inn," but "guestroom." Elsewhere in Luke, when he wrote of a paid lodging establishment, he used a different Greek word, *pandocheion*. For example, in the parable of the Good Samaritan, the wounded traveler was taken to a *pandocheion*, not a *kataluma*. Most English translations of the Bible say "there was no place for them in the inn" because that's the way we've always heard it. We imagine an innkeeper sending them away into the night. But according to biblical scholar Todd Bolen, it's not that there was no place for them in the inn; that Mary and Joseph arrived in Bethlehem late and the inn was full or that they couldn't afford a room. Rather, Bolen says, there was no room for them in the guestroom, meaning that Mary and Joseph were rejected by their own family.

Think about it. Bethlehem was Joseph's ancestral home. That's why he had to return there to register for the census. Isn't it likely that relatives were living in Bethlehem, and isn't it likely that Joseph expected to stay with them in the guestroom, the *kataluma*? The Common English Bible captures this distinction in its translation, "because there was no place for them in the guestroom" (Luke 2:7b). So, according to Bolen, not only were Mary and Joseph rejected by their families in Nazareth, but they also were rejected by their family in Bethlehem.[4] For this reason, Jesus was born in a barnyard.

His parents were poor and social outcasts. The circumstances of Jesus' birth were considered so shameful that no one wanted them. Can you imagine their desperation when Mary's labor pains began? There was no decent place for the baby to be born because even Mary and Joseph's own families did not want them. So, Jesus was born in the equivalent of a homeless shelter. At best it was a cave; at worst it was out in the open, under a starlit sky. Without a crib for a bed, Mary laid her newborn baby in a manger, a feeding trough for animals.

I've been thinking about the rejection Mary must have felt, the loneliness and the fear of having a baby with only Joseph by her side. Had she not known that her child was from God, I wonder how she could have endured. But soon others would come to share in her joy and to welcome her son. That very night shepherds would appear beside the manger, and later wise men would come from the East. Not everyone rejected Mary and Joseph and the baby. But rejection would become a theme in Jesus' life. John wrote in his gospel about Jesus: "His own people did not accept him" (1:11-12). And Jesus would later say of himself, "Foxes have holes and the birds of the air have nests, but the Son of Man has nowhere to lay his head" (Luke 9:58).

When Alberta Kirkpatrick first came to the Canterbury Shaker Village, she was lonely and afraid and almost at the point of giving up. She was an 11-year-old girl who had never known what it meant to be loved. But a Shaker sister in the village welcomed Alberta with open arms. The first time that Sister Marguerite Frost laid eyes on that timid, scared, emotionally scarred little girl, she ran up to Alberta and embraced her and hugged her and told her that she finally had a home. Sister Marguerite would become a kind of surrogate mother to Alberta—giving her the love, affection, and nurture she had desperately needed.

Alberta later learned that Sister Marguerite was feeling lonely herself before they met. It was the custom in the Shaker community for each member to receive one gift at Christmas. Only one gift—that is all anyone expected to receive. The Christmas before Alberta came to Canterbury, Sister Marguerite said the only gift she wanted was a little girl to love. And when Alberta arrived, to Sister Marguerite that little girl was the answer to her prayers. This is what Christmas is about.

Christmas is not about gorging ourselves with presents. Can you imagine being limited to only one Christmas gift? We want lots and lots of gifts under the tree with our name on them. But all the material things in the world cannot satisfy the deepest longings of our heart. What we really want, what we really need, is to be loved, to be wanted, to be accepted, to know we have some place in this world. And that is exactly what the coming of Jesus means: God loves us, God wants us, God accepts us, and God has a place for each of us in his family.

Material gifts are fun for a while, but what we really want, what we really need is love. We need God's love, we need the love of family and friends, and we need to love each other too. This world would be a lonely place without love. But God sent Jesus into the world to keep us from being lonely. As the poet Christina Rosetti wrote, "Love came down at Christmas."

There was no place for Mary and Joseph and the baby Jesus in Bethlehem, except for a manger. But because they knew that this child was a gift from God, even a barnyard became a sacred space, filled with a holy presence. At Christmas, God stepped down from heaven with a baby in his arms to tell us, to show us, we are loved. Love came down at Christmas, and the name of that love was Jesus.

THE REAL SPECTACLE OF CHRISTMAS
(Luke 2:1-7)

In November of 2009, Linda and I made a quick trip to Disney World in Florida. We stayed in the Animal Kingdom Lodge and spent two days at the Animal Kingdom theme park and one day at the Hollywood Studios theme park. We did not know much about the latter park, but we were impressed by the ambiance of the place. Many of the streets were like movie sets. We saw an Indiana Jones live stage show, and another stage show based on the Broadway musical, *Beauty and the Beast*. One street was made to look like an avenue in New York City. There were even mockups of the Empire State Building and the Chrysler Building at the end of the boulevard. As we were walking down that particular street, we noticed Christmas lights strung on all the buildings. We decided that if we were still in the park after dark, we would come back and see the lights lit up. Boy, were we in for a surprise!

Just after dark we went back to the New York City replica street. We were blown away by all the lights. It was spectacular! On that one street, about the equivalent of two city blocks, there were more than 5,000,000 Christmas lights—10 miles of strands, with 32 miles of extension cables. It seemed that every inch of every building was covered with lights. In addition to the strands of lights, there were twirling carousels suspended in the air, huge lighted Christmas trees on every corner, illuminated angels flying overhead, lighted marching toy soldiers, Santa and his reindeer in lights, a gigantic lighted globe spinning high above, and at least 43 illuminated Mickeys among the various displays.

Starting in mid-November and running every night until the first week in January, the lights were turned on at dusk. To add to the spectacle, Christmas music played through loudspeakers, and 66 snow machines on the roofs of the buildings pumped out artificial snow. It was like walking through a winter wonderland—except the night we were there, it was about 75 degrees. Thousands of people were just milling around, staring up in wonder as the lights flashed around them and the Christmas music played and the artificial snow fell on their faces. I even saw some people sticking out their tongues, trying to catch a few flakes. About every 15 minutes the lights would go out and the music would stop. A hushed anticipation would fall across the crowd. Then the Christmas music would start up again and the lights would come back on, flashing in rhythm with the music. At the end of the street, we saw a huge lighted display suspended over the road. The display read, "The Osborne Family Spectacle of Dancing Lights." We wondered: Who is the Osborne Family, and what do they have to do with the Christmas lights in a Disney theme park?

After we returned to Maryland, I did some research online and found out. It all began in 1986 at the home of Jennings and Mitzi Osborne in Little Rock, Arkansas. That year Jennings strung about 1,000 red lights on his house as a gift to their then-six-year-old daughter. The little girl was thrilled with the holiday display, so her daddy added to the lights every year after that. The display got so elaborate that the Osborne home was not big enough to hold all the lights, so Jennings purchased two properties next door to expand the light show. By 1993, the Osborne holiday light show had grown to 3,000,000 lights. It included a large spinning globe with Little Rock and Bethlehem illuminated in red; two rotating carousels of lights on each end of their circular driveway; a 70-foot-tall

Christmas tree with more than 80,000 lights mounted on the roof of their home; a canopy of 30,000 red lights over a section of the driveway; and more. Needless to say, the lights became a wildly popular attraction. People from all over Arkansas and neighboring states would drive to Little Rock to see the Osbornes' spectacle. Television camera crews came to film the display for news stories.

The Osborne family Christmas spectacle was not so popular with their neighbors, however. With traffic jams causing gridlock in the community, some neighbors filed suit in 1994 to have the display shut down. After a series of legal negotiations, Jennings Osborne agreed to a series of conditions, such as a set schedule for when the lights would be turned on and off each night, and hiring off-duty police officers to direct traffic and provide security. The uneasy truce lasted until one night when a family arrived at the display after the lights had been turned off. The disappointed family convinced Jennings Osborne to turn the lights back on. His act of generosity netted him a $10,000 fine for violating the terms of the court order. The neighbors went back to court and prevailed, with the judge ruling that the display be turned off permanently. Osborne appealed to the Arkansas Supreme Court and ultimately to the United States Supreme Court, where Justice Clarence Thomas refused to hear the case.

After the court rulings brought national media attention, a Walt Disney project director contacted the Osborne family attorney about the possibility of moving the massive display to one of their Orlando theme parks. Osborne accepted Disney's proposal, and beginning in 1995, the Osborne Family Spectacle of Dancing Lights became a popular holiday attraction at Disney World. It continued to grow every year until it was finally closed in January of 2016.

I did not know any of this as we walked up and down the boulevard marveling at all the lights. But we noticed at one end of the street, off to the side, there was a simple nativity scene, modestly lighted. I remarked to Linda that it would be easy to miss the nativity scene amid the spectacle of all the lights. But is not that what Christmas has become? The true meaning of Christmas has been relegated to a small display on a side street, while most of our attention is focused on staring at the pretty lights and dancing to the canned music and gazing up at the artificial snow.

The first Christmas could hardly have been more different from the Osborne spectacle. There were no dancing lights or loud piped-in music. There was a bright star in the sky, and there were angels singing over the fields outside town. But Jesus was born in a stable and laid in a feed trough for animals because there was no room for his family in the inn. Almost everything about that first Christmas was different from the spectacle that Christmas has become. No one expected the Messiah to be born in such humble circumstances. His mother was unmarried, a scandalous condition in those days. Mary was engaged to Joseph, who must have had to endure ridicule too. Jesus was born not only in scandal, but also in poverty. If Mary and Joseph had been people of means, they could have found some place to stay, even if there was no room for them in the inn. The whole nativity story is shot through with incongruity—the Son of God was born in the lowliest of conditions.

Because we know the story so well, the circumstances of the birth of Jesus are not shocking to us. But for people of his time, no one expected the Messiah to be born in such a humble state. He should have been born in a palace in Jerusalem, not in a stable in Bethlehem. His parents should have been royalty, not peasants. He should have been surrounded with wealth and luxury, not farm animals and the smell of the barnyard. Yet, that was the way God chose to send his Son into the world.

The 19th-century Danish philosopher and theologian Soren Kierkegaard tried to explain the seeming absurdity of Christmas, how "an infinite and eternal God became a finite and mortal man." Kierkegaard told the story of a mighty king who fell in love with a peasant girl. He wanted this young woman for his wife, but he was not sure how he should pursue her, a mere commoner. Should he travel in royal procession to her cottage and announce his arrival with blaring trumpets? Should he come to her wearing his royal crown and kingly robe and dazzle her with his wealth and power? Or should he simply demand that she become his wife—after all, he was the supreme sovereign of the realm, and he was entitled to any woman of his choosing. But then the king realized that if he pursued her in that way, he would never know if she truly loved him.

So, the king decided to set aside his crown, his kingly robes, his riches, and his power. If he were ever to know that she truly loved him, he would have to come to her as her equal. So, he came to her alone, dressed in tattered clothing as a beggar, seeking her acceptance, then her love. Is that not how God has come to us, as one of us? He set aside his glory and his power, and came as a humble, lowly child, born in a manger.

The word "spectacle" has two meanings. Spectacle can mean something grand and awesome, an impressive public display on a large scale, a marvel or wonder—for example, the Osborne Family Spectacle of Dancing Lights at Disney World. But spectacle has another meaning, as in the idiom "to make a spectacle" of oneself. God made a spectacle of himself in the way he chose to come into the world. At first appearing, it seems almost foolish for God to come into the world in that way—a scandalous pregnancy, an impoverished family, an unlikely venue, no room in the inn, no crib for a bed. Quite a spectacle, indeed, for the Son of God to be born that way! Yet, that is the real spectacle of Christmas. God became flesh and dwelt among us. And we beheld his glory, the glory of the Father's only Son, full of grace and truth.

QUESTIONS FOR DISCUSSION/REFLECTION

1. What was the significance of Jesus' being born in Bethlehem?
2. Can you imagine a mother today laying a newborn baby into a feed trough for animals? What would that say about her economic condition?
3. Why do you think there was no place for the Holy Family in the inn?
4. What is the meaning of Jesus' coming into the world in such humble circumstances?
5. There was no room for Jesus in the inn. Is there room for him in your heart?

NOTES

[1] *Time*, Dec. 23, 2013.
[2] *The Washington Post*, Dec. 12, 2013.
[3] Ibid., Dec. 17, 2013.
[4] "No Room in the Inn," Dec. 15, 2006, http://blog.bibleplaces.com.

CHAPTER 9

GOOD NEWS
(Luke 2:8-20)

"Don't be afraid! Look! I bring good news to you—wonderful, joyous news for all people. Your savior is born today in David's city. He is Christ the Lord." Suddenly a great assembly of the heavenly forces was with the angel praising God. "Glory to God in heaven, and on earth peace among those whom he favors."

(Luke 2:10-11, 13-14 CEB)

Perhaps you remember the lyric, "to certain poor shepherds," from "The First Nowell." One of my favorite Christmas carols, it was written in England in the 18th century or possibly earlier. The word "Nowell" comes from the French *noel*, meaning "birth announcement." The carol begins, "The first Nowell the angel did say, was to certain poor shepherds in fields as they lay."

There is a bit of a debate as to the meaning of the phrase, "to certain poor shepherds." Is "certain" an adjective, as in, to these particular shepherds, as opposed to other shepherds who might have been in the fields outside Bethlehem? Or is "certain" an archaic verb, as in, the first noel was given to "reassure" or to "make certain" to those poor shepherds in the fields that the angel came not to terrify them, but to bring them good news? Or maybe "certain" means that the poor shepherds were "certain," "sure," "confident" that the announcement of the birth of the baby in the manger was indeed good news of great joy. Maybe they were so certain of what the angel said that they left their flocks in the fields to go into Bethlehem to find the child and see for themselves what the Lord had made known to them.

THE SINGING OF ANGELS
(Luke 2:8-20)

I come from a musical family. My brother John is a piano professor in the music school at the University of North Carolina, Greensboro. My sister Carol was a music major in college. She had a beautiful soprano voice and starred in many musical productions in high school and college. We grew up with music in our home. There was often an album from a Broadway musical playing on the stereo in our living room, or a record from the innovative jazz musician Dave Brubeck. Our parents took us to hear classical music performed by the Fort Worth Symphony Orchestra, and to attend live musicals at the Casa Mañana Theatre. Then there was the music at church. I learned many of the hymns by heart. I sang in church choirs from preschool through high school. As a teenager I was a member of a musical ensemble called "The Saints." We sang religious and popular tunes, and even did a little choreography. I could not play the piano like my brother, or sing solos like my sister, but music was in my blood.

I don't know if the shepherds were musical or not. We do know that people sang and played musical instruments in biblical times. A thousand years before these shepherds, there was a shepherd boy named David. As a youth, long before he became king of Israel, David tended his father's sheep. When King Saul was troubled, he commanded his servants to find someone skillful in playing the lyre (1 Sam. 16:16). The idea was that when Saul was tormented by an evil spirit, the musician would play the lyre and Saul would feel better. Young David, the shepherd boy, was recruited to soothe Saul with the music of the lyre.

The lyre was a musical instrument whose sound was produced by plucking the strings with the fingers. It was used in both sacred and secular music and was played by Levites in the temple. In fact, many musical instruments are mentioned in the Bible. In addition to the lyre there were bells, castanets, cymbals, drums, flutes, harps, horns, pipes, tambourines (also called timbrels), and trumpets. So, there was a lot of music in biblical times.

The book of Psalms in the Old Testament is basically a hymnbook. It contains many of the songs that were sung in worship. Some of the psalms were ascribed to David, so he must have been both a poet and a musician. Although the shepherds in today's scripture lived many years after David, I can imagine that they passed the time watching their sheep while playing the music of a flute or a lute or a lyre, or just by singing. Music has a way of lifting the spirit and helping the time go by.

According to Luke 2, the shepherds were in the fields outside Bethlehem, "keeping watch over their flock by night. Then an angel of the Lord stood before them, and the glory of the Lord shone around them, and they were terrified. But the angel said to them, 'Do not be afraid, for see—I am bringing you good news of great joy for all the people: to you is born this day in the city of David, a Savior, who is the Messiah, the Lord. This will be a sign for you: you will find a child wrapped in bands of cloth and lying in a manger'" (2:8b-12, NRSV).

Professor Leon Morris, in his commentary on Luke in the Tyndale New Testament series, makes an intriguing observation about these shepherds. As a class of people, shepherds were not highly regarded. Because their work tending sheep kept them from observing all the ceremonial laws of the Jewish religion, they were considered unrighteous. And because they moved around a lot, anytime something was stolen, shepherds were the first to be accused of stealing. In fact, shepherds as a group were considered so unreliable that they were not allowed to give testimony in a court of law. It is somewhat surprising then that God should announce the birth of Jesus to such lowly people as shepherds, given their bad reputation.

But Morris notes that these shepherds were tending their flock in the fields outside Bethlehem. Most shepherds worked farther out in the wilderness, where most of the flocks were kept. Bethlehem was not far from Jerusalem. A rabbinic rule in the Mishnah specified that any sheep found between Jerusalem and a spot near Bethlehem was presumed to be an animal for sacrifice in the Temple. Professor Morris observes it was not unlikely that these shepherds were tending sheep destined for Temple sacrifices. Tending sheep intended for such a holy purpose may have sensitized these shepherds to the message they would receive from the angel.

So, these shepherds were the first to hear the birth announcement, and what an announcement it was! Born in Bethlehem was a Savior, the Messiah, the Lord. For centuries, the Jews had been waiting for a Savior—the Messiah, the "anointed one." Not only was this child the Savior and Messiah, but he also was "the Lord." "The Lord" was the term most frequently used for God. Thus, the angel described this child in the highest possible terms—Savior, Messiah, Lord. No wonder the angel said this was good news of great joy for all the people.

Suddenly, the angel was joined by a multitude of the heavenly host. That was where the music came in. They were singing praises to God: "Glory to God in the highest heaven, and on earth peace among those whom he favors" (Luke 2:14). Sometimes the spoken word is not enough to convey the message. Sometimes music is necessary. Music goes beyond the head, and into the heart. The angels sang that the coming of this Savior, the Messiah, the Lord, would bring peace—peace on earth, peace on those whom he favors.

Does this mean that God favors some people over others? Not at all! Jesus came for everyone. John said, "For God so loved the world that he gave his only Son, so that everyone who believes in him may not perish but may have eternal life" (John 3:16). Jesus came for everyone, but not everyone would receive God's favor. Peace with God comes through faith in Jesus. Peace on earth is God's gift in Jesus. The reason our world is still so far from peace on earth is because everyone in our world has yet to receive the gift of Jesus.

Some messages are too powerful to be spoken. They must be sung. The heavenly host sang praises to God and promised peace on earth to those whom he favors. God favors everyone, but we must accept God's favor. God will not impose himself on anyone. The shepherds understood that. They understood that they must respond to God's invitation. When the angels had left them, the shepherds said to one another, "'Let us go now to Bethlehem and see this thing that has taken place, that the Lord has made known to us.' So, they went with haste and found Mary and Joseph, and the child lying in the manger" (Luke 2:15b-16, NRSV).

Earlier, I said I did not know if the shepherds in this story were musical or not. But on a closer reading of the text, I believe they were. At the end of the story, after seeing Jesus in the manger, "the shepherds returned, glorifying and praising God for all they had heard and seen" (Luke 2:20a). After having met the Christ child, face to face, how could they keep from singing?

Have you ever had a song get into your mind and just rattle around in there, as if it won't leave? That happens to me from time to time. I'll hear a song and it will stick with me. I'll wake up in the middle of the night and realize I had been hearing that song or even singing it in my dreams. But this was no dream for the shepherds. This was their new reality. They had heard angels singing. They had seen the reason for the angels' song. That's what the birth of Jesus does for us, when we believe. It puts a song of joy in our hearts. It gives us a song that we will sing for the rest of our lives. And when our life on earth is over, we will join the angels and sing with joy in heaven.

In his book, *For the Inward Journey*, Howard Thurman, wrote these words:

> There must be … in every life some place for the singing of angels—some place for that which…is breathlessly beautiful … —something that gathers up … all the freshets of experience from drab and commonplace areas of living and glows in one bright light of penetrating beauty and meaning …. The commonplace is shot through with new glory—old burdens become lighter, deep and ancient wounds lose much of their old, old hurting. A crown is placed over our heads that for the rest of our lives we are trying to grow tall enough to wear. Despite all the crassness of life, despite all the hardness of life, despite all the harsh discords of life, life is saved by the singing of angels.[1]

I don't know if you are musical or not, but I do know that Jesus came to put a song in your heart. Amid all the crassness, hardness, and harsh discords of life, life is saved by the singing of angels.

WHEN THE SONG OF THE ANGELS IS STILLED
(Luke 2:7-20)

My wife Linda collects crèches, sometimes called nativities. I define a "crèche" or "nativity" as having at least Mary, Joseph, and the baby Jesus in it. Some nativities include the manger and the shepherds. Some have animals alongside. Some crèches include the wise men, although they were not there the night when Jesus was born. (They came later when Jesus and his parents were living in a house.) Still, the wise men were a part of the story of the birth of Jesus, so I don't mind if some nativity scenes place the wise men at the manger too. Crèches are beautiful, but they probably are not accurate depictions of the scene.

I don't know if you have been in a stable lately, or spent much time around barnyard animals, but it's generally not as pristine as those nativity scenes. A stable is usually dirty and smelly and a far cry from sanitary. And I can imagine that when Mary gave birth in the stable, it was not so pretty and peaceful as most nativity scenes depict it.

Yet, my guess is that eventually it became a quiet place when all the commotion from the night before had passed. The pains of birth were over. The song of the angels was stilled. The shepherds had come and gone. By dawn's early light, only Mary and Joseph were there, watching the baby in the manger, asleep on the hay. Mary was likely in a reflective mood. Luke says that Mary treasured these things and pondered them in her heart (2:19). And that's what we are left to do when Christmas has passed. We reflect upon what the coming of Jesus means for our lives.

First, notice the circumstances of his birth. Jesus, the Messiah, the anointed one, the King, was born not in a palace but in a barnyard. He was born not in earthly riches but in earthly poverty. The circumstances of his birth foreshadowed his mission—namely, to bring good news to the poor, release to the captives, recovery of sight to the blind, to let the oppressed go free. Later, in the synagogue in Nazareth near the beginning of his public ministry, Jesus would read this prophecy from Isaiah aloud. It was like his mission statement. He said, "Today this prophecy has been fulfilled in your hearing" (Luke 4:21). For the rest of his life, Jesus went about fulfilling that mission. He had a heart for all people, but especially for the poor, the sick, the downtrodden, the oppressed. The Gospels are filled with stories of Jesus reaching out to the lowly, the marginalized, the outcasts, the people that the religious leaders had little use for. His humble birth in a stable in Bethlehem, his manger bed, was a precursor for his life. Jesus was born in earthly poverty, and he would live in humble circumstances. He had no place of his own. During his ministry Jesus would say, "Foxes have holes and birds of the air have nests, but the Son of Man has nowhere to lay his head" (Matt. 8:20).

The example of Jesus' ministry says to me that if we would follow Jesus, we also must have a heart for "the least of these," as he called them in his parable. The fact that the good news of Jesus' birth was first announced to lowly shepherds, rather than to King Herod or the chief priests or other high and mighty persons, is a sign of what we should be about.

Dietrich Bonhoeffer was a German Lutheran pastor who got involved in the resistance to the Nazis and Adolph Hitler during the Second World War. Eventually Bonhoeffer was arrested for his participation in a plot that attempted to assassinate Hitler. Following his arrest, Bonhoeffer wrote these words in a letter from prison:

> Misery, sorrow, poverty, loneliness, helplessness, and guilt mean something different in the eyes of God than according to human judgment; that God turns toward the very places from which humans turn away; that Christ was born in a stable because there was no room for him in the inn—a prisoner grasps this better than others. And for them, this is truly good news.[2]

Jesus was born in a stable and laid in a manger as a sign that God cares for the lowly. His humble birth circumstance is a summons for us to care for the poor, the prisoners, the underserved, and the forgotten.

Second, notice that the birth of Jesus is good news of great joy for all the people. It is not only a summons to serve, but also an invitation to sing for joy. The church is far more than a social service agency. It is a celebration of what God has done in Jesus Christ and what God continues to do in our individual lives and our life together. Unto us is born a Savior, who is the Messiah, the Lord. When we accept Jesus as our Savior and make him the Lord of our lives, we discover a deeper joy and a greater purpose in life.

Rejoicing is at the very heart of the Christmas story. The angels sang "Glory to God," and the shepherds returned to their fields glorifying and praising God. This is good news of great joy! In Jesus, God came to draw us to himself. In Jesus, God came to reconcile us to himself. Though our sins have separated us from God, God so loved the world that he gave his only Son, that whoever believes in him may not perish, but may have eternal life (John 3:16).

Third, notice that the birth of Jesus is not only about peace with God, but also about peace with each other. Jesus came to bring peace to our hearts, but he also came to bring peace to our world. And the way that Jesus brings peace to our world is through people. We live in a time of great divisiveness—political, racial, economic, and religious divisions. As followers of Jesus, we are called to be peacemakers. We are called to share the love of Christ with all people, and to seek to build bridges of understanding and mutual respect so that there may be peace on earth.

One Christmas our daughter-in-law Stacey gave Linda and me a book with blank pages on which we were to write about our lives. The idea was to record some of our memories so that one day, when our granddaughter Ford is older, she might read it. For the following year, every time Stacey would see us, she would ask if we had started on the book. Her consistent prompting got Linda to start consistently prompting me. Finally, I wrote my part in the book. Then Linda finished her part of the book, including pasting in many family photos.

The book was a series of questions intended to promote reflection and reminiscing. One of the questions was, "What is the best gift you have ever received?" Well, for me, the best gifts I have ever received are people: my wife Linda, our daughter Amy, our son Marc, our daughter-in-law Stacey, and our granddaughter Ford. When Linda and I got married, it was one of the best days of my life. I'll never forget little four-year-old Amy walking down the aisle ahead of her mother. My heart was lifted up.

Another best day of my life was when Marc was born. It was early in the morning at Holy Cross Hospital in Silver Spring, Maryland. I was with Linda while she was labor, but when they wheeled her into the delivery room, I went into the waiting room. For about an hour, I sat there by myself. The hospital can be a quiet place at 3:00 in the morning. After not hearing anything for what seemed like an eternity, I started wondering if everything were okay. Finally, someone came out and told me that Linda and the baby were fine. I rushed out into the hallway and turned the corner, and there they were, lying on a gurney in the hospital corridor. My heart was lifted up.

Another best day of my life was when Marc and Stacey got married. The wedding site was a community garden in New York City. I did not officiate, but they asked me— along with Stacey's dad—to say a few words during the ceremony. My mother was there, Amy was there, Linda was there, Stacey's family was there, and my heart was lifted up.

Several years later, Marc called from California to tell us that Stacey was in labor. He asked us if we wanted him to call again after the baby was born, even if it were the middle of the night. Duh? Call? Well, he did call about 3:30 the next morning. Stacey and the baby were fine. Our hearts were lifted up. Then he told us their daughter's name—Ford. That was Linda's maiden name. She was Linda Ford. Linda and I sat together on the side of the bed at 3:30 in the morning and we cried tears of joy.

I imagine there were tears of joy the night when Jesus was born. He was the best gift that Mary and Joseph would ever receive. He was also the best gift that the shepherds would ever receive. Jesus was the best gift that the world would ever receive.

So, here we are reflecting on what this gift means for us, pondering these things in our hearts. For me, Christmas means that we are called to serve others in Christ's name. Christmas means we rejoice, and praise God, and sing for joy. Christmas means that we seek to make peace in our world. It means that when we receive this greatest gift, we find that our hearts are lifted up too.

One of my favorite authors, Howard Thurman, wrote this poem in his book, *The Mood of Christmas*:

When the song of the angels is stilled,
When the star in the sky is gone,
When the kings and the princes are home,
When the shepherds are back with their flocks,
The work of Christmas begins:
To find the lost,
To heal the broken,
To feed the hungry,
To release the prisoner,
To rebuild the nations,
To bring peace among brothers,
To make music in the heart.[3]

When we talk about the birth of Jesus, we say "Merry Christmas!" Except, Christmas is better than that. Christmas is much better than merry. God is with us. Rejoice! Christ the Savior is born.

SAVIOR, MESSIAH, LORD
(Luke 2:8-14)

There is a church on the west side of Nashville in a low-income neighborhood known as "The Nations." More than 90 percent of the children in the surrounding community qualify for free or reduced-price school lunches. The church itself is small, numbering just over 100 members. Most of the congregants are low-income themselves, including several members who are homeless. Since 1993, Highland Park Church—in partnership with the United Methodist churches, the Davidson County Sheriff's Office, and the United States Marine Reserve Toys for Tots—has provided Christmas gifts to families in need. For almost 30 years that little Methodist church on the west side of Nashville has opened its "Last Minute Toy Store" the week before Christmas. The "store" is a room in the church filled with donated new toys. That little church on the west side of Nashville understands what Christmas is about. It's about gifts for children, to be sure, but Christmas is about more than that. It's about good news to the poor, about caring concern for "the least" of God's people.

Our scripture passage could hardly be more familiar. Just about everyone knows the story. Mary and Joseph were strangers in town when they came to Bethlehem. There was no room for them in the inn. Because they had no place to stay, and it was almost time for Mary to give birth, they were desperate for shelter. They found refuge in a barnyard. When Jesus was born, they laid him in a manger, a feed box for animals, because there was no crib for a bed. Talk about humble beginnings! The family of Jesus was basically homeless.

We are not shocked by these circumstances because we know them so well. In fact, we have romanticized the scene with our nativity crèches and Christmas carols to the point that it's almost quaint and sentimental. We have made the story so sweet and tender that we have missed the hardship and scandal of it. Jesus was born in poverty, not in a palace! His parents were peasants, not royalty or religious elite. His humble birth was a foreshadowing of his humble life and his scandalous death. Years later, as an adult, Jesus would say, "the Son of Man came not to be served but to serve, and to give his life as a ransom for many" (Matt. 20:28). That's what the manger represents—humility, service, self-giving, sacrificial love. The humility of Jesus' birth was a foreshadowing of the scandal of his death. Over the manger hangs the specter of a cross. What is implicit in his birth will become explicit in his death. Paul described it in his letter to the Philippians:

> Let the same mind be in you that was in Christ Jesus, who, though he was in the form of God, did not regard equality with God as something to be exploited, but emptied himself, taking the form of a slave, being born in human likeness. And being found in human form, he humbled himself and became obedient to the point of death—even death on a cross. (Phil. 2:5-8, NRSV)

Not only was the place where Jesus was born surprising, but the birth announcement also was surprising. Angels announced his birth—we are not surprised by that. But the people to whom they announced his birth were not who we would expect to be the first to hear the good news. Shouldn't the angels have appeared to King Herod, or to the High Priest in the Temple, or to the Sanhedrin, or even to Caesar Augustus? Why would the angels come to lowly shepherds? They weren't important at all. In fact, shepherds were so unimportant that their testimony was not admissible in a court of law. Who could trust the word of a shepherd? Uneducated, uncultured, ritually unclean, poor, and with unsavory reputations—there could hardly have been more unlikely witnesses to the birth of Jesus. Was God trying to tell us something here?

Jesus was born in poverty, and his birth was announced to the lowest strata of society. Maybe it was God's way of saying that Jesus came to turn the values of the world upside down. The angel said this baby, born to poor parents in a back alley of Bethlehem, wrapped in strips of cloth and laid in a feed trough for animals, was none other than their Savior, the Messiah, the Lord. Let's unpack those titles the angel gave to the baby Jesus.

First, Savior: the very name "Jesus" means "God will save." When the angel appeared to Joseph in a dream the angel said, "you are to name him Jesus, for he will save his people from their sins." Jesus came to be our Savior, to save us from our sins. And is there any question that we need to be saved? Look at the state our world is in right now. There is so much violence, injustice, and greed, and inhumanity that we have almost become accustomed to it. Of course, some sins are more obvious and egregious than others. But just because we haven't killed someone or robbed a bank, let us not imagine that we are without sin. Paul wrote to the Romans, "all have sinned and fall short of the glory of God" (Rom. 3:23). The very fact that there are so many poor people throughout our land is testimony to the economic injustices of our society. Let us not imagine that a few charitable deeds make up for a culture that is characterized by greed and neglectful materialism. And let us not become so morally self-righteous that we think our good deeds can save us. Jesus came to save not just obvious and egregious sinners, but to save smugly religious sinners too.

The second title given to the baby Jesus was Messiah, or as it comes from the Greek, Christ. It's not a surname. We are so used to hearing the names together, Jesus Christ, that we forget that Christ, or Messiah, means "anointed." Jesus was anointed to do God's work in the world. In the Old Testament, kings were anointed with God's Spirit and power to serve God and do his will. Jesus the Messiah, or Jesus the Christ, means that he came to establish an eternal kingdom of justice and righteousness and truth. Of course, Jesus was not the kind of Messiah the Jews were looking for. They were expecting a military Messiah who would defeat their enemies by force. They were expecting the Messiah to annihilate sinners, not to forgive them. They certainly were not expecting the Messiah to suffer violence and die like a common criminal.

Third, the angel called Jesus "the Lord," meaning the one who is in charge. In the Roman Empire, Caesar was Lord. People even worshipped the emperor as a "god." But the angel announced the birth of one who would become the true emperor of the world and who would bring true peace, not through the sword but through the cross. If Jesus indeed is our Lord, he has authority over every aspect of our lives. He has authority over not only what we do in church, but also over what we do with the rest of our lives. If Jesus is Lord, then he is Lord of our finances, Lord of our jobs, Lord of our family life, Lord of our leisure time, Lord of our politics, Lord of our ambitions, Lord of all we think and do and say. If an angel had not told the shepherds, they never would have believed it. That baby in a manger, that poor little Jesus boy, was Savior, Messiah, and Lord.

There is a story from Brazil about a girl named Christina and her mother Maria. Christina's father died when she was just an infant, and Maria struggled to raise her daughter on her own. Maria was never able to provide Christina with the luxuries of life, but she kept a roof over her head, and clothes on her back, and food in her stomach. But Christina was not satisfied. She imagined a better world was in the glamorous streets of Rio de Janeiro. So, one day without even saying goodbye, Christina left the dusty streets of the only neighborhood she had ever known for the bright lights of the big city.

When Maria discovered that Christina was gone, she was heartbroken. Maria had done everything she could for her daughter, and this is how she was repaid? But Maria would not give up on her child. Maria threw some clothes in a bag, gathered up all her money, and left for Rio. On her way to the bus stop she stopped by a drugstore for one last thing. Maria climbed into a photo booth, pulled the curtain to, and then spent all she could on pictures of herself. She stuffed the small black-and-white photos into her purse as she boarded the bus to Rio.

Maria knew that Christina would end up in a bad part of the city. Because Christina had only a basic education and no marketable skills, Maria feared her daughter would end up selling herself just to survive. So, Maria began to search for her daughter in bars, cheap hotels, nightclubs, and other such places. Everywhere she went, Maria left a small picture of herself, taped to bathroom mirrors, tacked on hotel bulletin boards, fastened to bus stop benches. On the back of each photo Maria wrote a note. Failing to find her daughter, and with her funds exhausted, Maria boarded a bus to go back to her small village.

Some days later, Christina was coming down the stairs of a seedy hotel when she saw a small photo with a familiar face. The glamour of the big city was far gone by now. Her dream of freedom had become a nightmare. Her spirit was broken. But as she walked across the room and removed the small photo of her mother from the wall, her eyes filled with tears. Holding the photo in her trembling hand, she turned it over to read the words her mother had written: "Whatever you have done, whatever you have become, I love you. Please come home." And that's what she did.

God left a photo of himself in this world. In the birth and life and death and resurrection of Jesus, we see the Father's heart. John wrote in his gospel: "No one has ever seen God. It is God the only Son, who is close to the Father's heart, who has made him known" (1:18). Jesus said, "Whoever has seen me has seen the Father" (14:9). What we see in Jesus is what we get in God. In Jesus, God says to each of us: "Whatever you have done, whatever you have become, I love you. Please come home."

QUESTIONS FOR DISCUSSION/REFLECTION

1. Why did the angel announce the good news to shepherds?
2. What is the significance of the Savior, Christ the Lord, lying in a manger?
3. Has God ever sent an angel to you with a message?
4. How can we glorify and praise God for what he has done?
5. In what ways is this wonderful, joyous news for all people?

NOTES

[1] Howard Thurman, *For the Inward Journey* (Friends United Press, 1984), 247.
[2] Dietrick Bonhoeffer, *Letters and Papers from Prison* (Fortress Press, 2010), 225.
[3] Howard Thurman, *The Mood of Christmas* (Friends United Press, 1973), 23.

CHAPTER 10

THE WORD BECAME FLESH
(John 1:1-18)

> *In the beginning was the Word, and the Word was with God, and the Word was God. And the Word became flesh and lived among us, and we have seen his glory, the glory as of a father's only son, full of grace and truth.* (John 1:1, 14, 18 NRSV)

No one has ever seen God. Yet in Jesus, we have seen the Word made flesh, the Word that was with God and the Word that was God. We call it "the Incarnation." The invisible God became incarnate through his Son. The prologue to John's gospel is not a Christmas story, per se, but it is the story behind the Christmas story. The Word, *logos* in the Greek, is more than speech. It is God expressing himself. In Genesis, God spoke and Creation came into being. John said the Word was the agent of creation. Jesus was the Word made flesh. In Jesus, God's glory dwelt in human form. Such glory was full of grace and truth. God the Son made God the Father known.

As I was approaching retirement from the full-time pastorate, I had to select a scripture text for my final sermon at Village Baptist Church. After 33 years at the same church, what more could I say? I selected John 1:14-18, and titled the sermon, "God's Love Made Visible." My closing message to the congregation was simply this: In Jesus, God's love is made visible. I included that sermon in my book, *Preaching for the Long Haul: A Case Study on Long-term Pastoral Ministry*. I also included in that book three other sermons based on the prologue to John's gospel. There is always more to say.

NO ONE HAS EVER SEEN GOD
(Exod. 33:17-23, John 1:17-18)

Our friend Pete Parreco picked us up about 7 a.m. on a Tuesday morning and took us to Thurgood Marshall BWI Airport where we boarded a nonstop flight for Seattle. After arriving in Seattle and retrieving our bags from the luggage carousel, Linda and I walked about a block to the subway station where we boarded a railcar for downtown. Once downtown, we walked another block to the train station, where we boarded a bus for Vancouver. After about a three-hour bus ride to downtown Vancouver, we hailed a taxi to our hotel. By the time we checked in, it was 11 p.m. Pacific Daylight Time, or 2 a.m. Eastern Standard Time. The next morning, we took a shuttle from the hotel to the harbor where we boarded the ship to begin our voyage to Alaska.

If all this traveling sounds arduous, consider Moses and the Israelites on their journey to the Promised Land. They did not have cars or airplanes or subways or buses or taxis or cruise ships. They walked, and it was a long and dangerous trek. Moses wanted God to guide them, to show his face and lead the way. God did provide a cloud by day and a pillar of fire by night, but God would not show his face. No one can look at the face of God and live. The closest Moses came to seeing God was when God put Moses in the cleft of the rock and covered the place with his hand. As God passed by, Moses got a glimpse, not of God's face, but of God's backside. That was as close as Moses was allowed to get. As John said in the first chapter of his gospel, "No one has ever seen God."

We did not see the face of God in Alaska, but we saw plenty of signs of God's handiwork. As we cruised the inner passage, we saw lush, forested shorelines, towering snow-capped mountains, and rushing waterfalls along the Canadian coast. The magnificence was mesmerizing. Once we finally got off the ship and ventured beyond the quaint town of Ketchikan, there was beauty all around us. Because southeast Alaska gets a lot of rainfall, the trees are so thick that only moss can grow on the forest floor. Ketchikan gets 142 inches of rain a year. Compare that with Seattle's 35 inches.

With all that rain, we saw a lot of trees—Western Hemlock, Sitka Spruce, cedar, pine, birch, aspen, poplar. With an economy based on tourism and commercial fishing, Ketchikan is called the "Salmon Capital of the World." We felt right at home. We saw a boy catch a salmon while fishing off a bridge. Another boy climbed down the rocks to retrieve a salmon that had miscalculated its jump and ended up on the riverbank. I asked the boy what he was going to do with the big fish. He said, "I'm going to eat it!"

Our journey by ship continued up the Alaskan coast. We stopped in Juneau and took a bus to see the Mendenhall Glacier. Then we took a tram to the top of Mount Roberts. The next day, a Sunday, we stopped in Skagway where Linda and I attended a Presbyterian church. We spent the next two days on the ship cruising through Glacier Bay and College Fjord. The ship stopped in front of Margerie Glacier in Glacier Bay for about an hour. We watched as the glacier calved, dropping large chunks of ice into the sea. It was almost a religious experience.

We did not see the face of God in Alaska, but we saw plenty of evidence of God. After we got off the ship in Whittier, we took a nine-hour train ride to Denali National Park and Preserve. What makes Denali unique among the national parks is that the ecosystem is almost intact. There is only one road into Denali, and it is paved just a portion of the way. Vehicular traffic is limited to tour buses and a few campers and cars. Within an area of six million acres, larger than the state of New Hampshire, there are only a few established trails. The habitat of Denali has been preserved. No rivers have been diverted. No effort has been given to manage the wildlife. No value judgments are made between predators and prey. Wildlife populations are self-regulating. At one time, when the Dall sheep seemed in peril, some employees of the National Park Service argued for predator control. They were afraid the sheep would become extinct. But others argued that predators are what keep the ecosystem in balance. That vision has prevailed. There is no herd management or predator regulation at Denali.

Wolves and bears hunt freely. Wolves can travel up to 50 miles a day on the prowl for food. When they hunt large animals such as caribou, the wolves target the young, the old, the weak, and the sick. It is a classic case of survival of the fittest. The mortality rate for snowshoe hares and voles is frightfully high. Ground squirrels have threats on every side. They are hunted by wolves, lynx, foxes, wolverines, golden eagles, and grizzly bears. Those poor ground squirrels must live in a state of perpetual anxiety. Some can rest in winter, but only if they find a safe place to hibernate. Caribou calves are able to walk an hour after birth, and able to run with the herd just a day or two later. That is the only way the young caribou can hope to survive hungry bears who have emerged from their dens and ravenous wolves who are feeding their young. Even the mighty moose are vulnerable. Just one moose calf out of 10 will survive its first year. Many predators also die for lack of food or other harsh conditions in the wild.

The winters in Denali are so severe, it's a wonder anything can survive. Air temperatures can reach 50, 60, 70 degrees below zero. And that's not counting the wind chill. Average annual snowfall in Denali is 195 inches, or 16 feet! Rangers use sled dogs to get around the park, rather than snowmobiles (or "snow machines," as they call them). Huskies pull sleds a thousand miles each winter as rangers patrol the park. Only a few hearty souls spend the winter in Denali.

When we were at the Denali Visitors' Center, Linda and I watched a wonderful film about the park. Near the end of the film a quotation appeared on the movie screen. The quotation was from an environmentalist named Terry Tempest Williams, a scholar in environmental humanities at the University of Utah. Williams has written several books, such as *Finding Beauty in a Broken World*. She also has written articles for *The New Yorker, The New York Times*, and *Orion* magazine. Widely known as an advocate for ecological consciousness and social change, Williams is quoted near the end of the film, saying: "If we listen to the land, we will know what to do."

"If we listen to the land, we will know what to do." I think I understand what that quotation means. I think Williams was trying to say that we should take care of the land. We should respect the rhythms of nature and not upset the fragile balance of the ecosystem. We should be concerned about global warming and the other consequences of human activity. If that is what Terry Tempest Williams meant to say, I agree with it. "If we listen to the land, we will know what to do."

But there is another level, a deeper level to life, than simply having respect for nature. Frankly, just listening to the land does not tell us what to do in those deeper levels of living. I suppose, in some sense, God does speak to us through nature. But if nature were all we had to go on, I'm not sure we would know what to do. Nature can be beautiful and inspiring, but nature can also be harsh and unforgiving. There is a reason why less than 800,000 people live in the vast state of Alaska. And if we follow the examples of the natural world, human life would be pretty ruthless and inhumane. Who wants to live in a world where only the strong survive? To a limited degree, God does speak to us through nature. But God's voice, God's ultimate word, comes to us not through the land, but through his Son. As John said, "No one has ever seen God. It is God the only Son, who is close to the Father's heart, who has made him known." We will know what to do, not just by listening to the land, but by listening to God's Word, and preeminently God's Word made flesh in God's only Son.

At the center of Denali National Park and Preserve is the tallest mountain in North America, Mount McKinley. The odd thing about this mountain is that most visitors to Denali never get to see it. You would think it would be easy to see. But most of the time, its summit is shrouded in clouds. When I asked our guide why, she replied that it is because Mount McKinley creates its own weather system. Of all the visitors to Denali, we were told that only 30 percent ever catch a glimpse of the mighty mountain, and only 10 percent get to see it clearly.

Well, we were among the 10 percent. The clouds broke, and we saw the mountain in all its glory. It was a thrilling sight. The mountain rises more than 20,000 feet. Five glaciers flow down its sides. Our guide kept telling us how fortunate we were to see the mountain so clearly. I wished we had a better camera, but Linda and I were snapping pictures with our cellphones as fast as we could. For a few glorious minutes, we saw the top of the mountain that the indigenous peoples call Denali, which means "the great one."

No one has ever seen "the Great One." No one has ever seen God. But in Jesus Christ we have seen what God looks like in human form. In the life of Jesus, the clouds surrounding the mystery of God parted. Moses hid in the cleft of the rock and only saw the backside as God passed by. But we who stand at the foot of the cross can see God face to face. "The Word became flesh and lived among us, and we have seen his glory, the glory as of a father's only son, full of grace and truth" (John 1:14). If we listen to Jesus, we will know what to do.

WHO IS JESUS?
(John 1:1-18)

Reza Aslan is author of the best-selling book, *Zealot: The Life and Times of Jesus of Nazareth*. When he wrote the book Aslan was an associate professor of creative writing at the University of California, Riverside. His book about Jesus became a bestseller for several reasons. One, it is well written. It was designed for a general audience, so it is not nearly as dry and technical as more academic works. Two, Dr. Aslan is a Muslim. A Muslim writing a book about Jesus is somewhat unusual. Three, interest in the book increased dramatically after Aslan was interviewed on Fox television by news host Lauren Green. A clip from the interview went viral on the Internet, and Aslan became almost famous. In the interview Green repeatedly asked Aslan why he as a Muslim chose to write a book about Jesus. The implication of her questions seemed to be that a Muslim writing a book about Jesus must be part of some nefarious plot to undermine the Christian faith.

I have not read Reza Aslan's book, but I've read excerpts and almost a dozen reviews of the book, many by people I highly respect. Some of the reviewers are biblical scholars who know a lot more about the life and times of Jesus of Nazareth than Reza Aslan does. One reviewer said that Aslan is more of a reader than a researcher. Instead of doing actual historical research into the life and times of Jesus, he read about the research that historians and biblical scholars have done, and he cherry-picked the parts that supported his thesis that Jesus of Nazareth was a zealot.

What makes the book intriguing is the background of the author. Reza Aslan was born in Iran. His family fled to the United States after the regime change in 1979. Aslan said he was Muslim in much the same way that he was Persian. His religion and his ethnicity were tied together. He was born into a religious tradition, but his family was not particularly devout. After the revolution in Iran, religion in general, and Islam in particular, became almost taboo subjects in his home. Aslan says that "Islam was shorthand for everything we had lost to the mullahs who now ruled Iran." His mother still prayed when no one was looking, but after they came to America, for the most part, all talk about religion was avoided. That was fine with Reza, because being a Muslim in America in the 1980s was like being from Mars. As an immigrant, he wanted to fit in with American culture—not stand out.

The summer after his sophomore year in high school, Reza was invited to a church camp in northern California. During the day the campers roamed the outdoors, played games, sang songs, and enjoyed having fun together. In the evenings everyone gathered in the fire-lit assembly hall for evangelical worship. There, Reza first heard a remarkable story that would change his life forever. He heard that 2,000 years ago in a land called Galilee there lived a man named Jesus. He was no ordinary man but was the Son of God. Through his words and actions Jesus challenged the religious leaders of his day, and in return he was nailed to a cross. His death was not just a miscarriage of justice but was the atoning sacrifice that would free humanity from the burden of sin. But the story did not end there. Three days later Jesus rose from the grave, and his resurrection means all who believe and accept him into their hearts will have eternal life.

This is the story that Reza Aslan heard for the first time at church camp in northern California. He believed that it was the greatest story ever told. He said that for a kid raised in a "motley family of lukewarm Muslims and exuberant atheists," he had never before felt the pull of God so intimately. Not only did Jesus seem to fill a hole in his heart, but becoming a Christian was as close as he could get to feeling truly American. It was not just a conversion of convenience. Reza burned with devotion to his newfound faith. As soon as he returned home from church camp, he began sharing the good news of Jesus with his family and friends. Reza became a zealot in his own right, but his zeal did not last long.

As he began to study the Bible, the deeper he probed into the life of Jesus, the more questions his study raised. In college he began to study other religions, and his questions about the Christian faith "ballooned into full-blown doubts." The more he read and thought about it, the more confused he became. Eventually, he angrily discarded his Christian faith as if it were a costly forgery that he had been duped into buying. Feeling spiritually unmoored, he began to rethink the faith and culture of his Persian heritage. Finally, he converted back to being a Muslim. In 2005 he wrote a book about Islam titled *No god but God* that became an international bestseller and was translated into 13 languages. Given his own spiritual pilgrimage, in which he embraced Christianity, and then left the Christian faith, one might wonder why Reza Aslan would write a book about Jesus.

Of course, books about Jesus are nothing new. Thousands of books about Jesus are written every year. In 1906 Albert Schweitzer, the famous missionary doctor in Africa, published a book in German known by its English title, *The Quest of the Historical Jesus*.

In the book Schweitzer reviewed more than two centuries of studies about the historical Jesus. Schweitzer began his review with an 18th-century German philosopher named Hermann Samuel Reimarus who wrote about his own investigation of the historical Jesus. Schweitzer's book covered subsequent attempts to discover the historical Jesus, leading to his own analysis written at the beginning of the 20th century. I've read part of Schweitzer's book, and while it is scholarly and erudite, I wouldn't recommend it, unless you are looking to read a book before bedtime that will put you to sleep. But the point is, "the quest of the historical Jesus" has been going on a long time.

Who is Jesus? This is an important question for us to seek to answer, because Jesus is the focus of the Christian faith. Of course, the ultimate focus of our faith is God, but as Christians, we believe that Jesus is the unique and definitive revelation of God. In other words, most of what we believe about God comes from what we know of Jesus. Without Jesus, our knowledge of God would be extremely limited. Plus, in my Baptist denomination, Jesus is the criterion by which we interpret scripture. We don't have a pope or creeds or religious authorities to tell us how to understand the scriptures. We have Jesus, the Living Word of God, and he is the key to interpreting the written Word of God. Not every part of the Bible is of equal relevance to our lives. The dietary laws of the Old Testament are of far less importance to us than the teachings of Jesus in the New Testament. That's why is it crucial for us to know who Jesus is—what he taught, what he did, what he stood for, and how he wants us to live as we seek to follow him.

There is a parable told in the Dostoyevsky novel, *The Brothers Karamazov*, called "The Grand Inquisitor." In the parable Jesus returns to earth during the time of the Spanish Inquisition. He performs miracles, much as he did in the Bible, and the people recognize him and believe in him, but the Inquisition leaders have him arrested. He is sentenced to be burned at the stake the next day. The Grand Inquisitor comes to visit Jesus in his prison cell the night before his scheduled execution. The Grand Inquisitor tells Jesus that the Church no longer needs him. The Grand Inquisitor explains to Jesus that his return is disruptive with what the leaders of the church are trying to do. The inquisitors see their mission as instructing people how to believe and what to do, but Jesus is interfering with that by offering people freedom to choose for themselves. The Grand Inquisitor does not think that most people can handle the freedom Jesus is giving them. Jesus remains silent throughout the whole interrogation. After being lambasted for not speaking up for himself, Jesus' only response is to stand up, walk over to the Grand Inquisitor, and kiss him. Upon being kissed by Jesus, the Grand Inquisitor releases him, but tells Jesus never to return. Jesus, still silent, walks out into "the dark alleys of the city." The parable calls us to wonder what would happen if Jesus showed up today. Would we recognize him and believe in him and follow him, or would we reject him because he bears little resemblance to our preconceptions about Jesus? Would we see Jesus as a disruption to our lives, or would we seek to be more like him?

Reza Aslan draws a distinction between the Jesus of history and the Christ of faith, saying that Christians have made the Christ of faith into their own image, rather than following the Jesus of history. Like many other "questers" before him, Aslan claims to have unveiled the true Jesus of history rather than the manmade Christ of faith. But more than a hundred years ago, Albert Schweitzer recognized that every so-called "life of Jesus" resembles its author more than its subject matter. Obviously, the Bible does not tell us everything about the life of Jesus. Schweitzer said, "from these materials [meaning the four Gospels] we only get a Life of Jesus with yawning gaps." Schweitzer asked, "How are these gaps to be filled?"[1]

The answer is that we fill the yawning gaps by coming to know Jesus for ourselves. As John said in our scripture, "No one has ever seen God." It is "God the only Son, who is close to the Father's heart, who has made him known." The more we read about Jesus, the more we think about what he said and did, the more we seek to follow him in the way we live, the more we come to know him, the closer we come to the Father's heart.

At the end of *The Quest of the Historical Jesus*, Albert Schweitzer wrote these words:

He comes to us as One unknown, without a name, as of old, by the lake-side, He came to those men who knew Him not. He speaks to us the same word: "Follow me!" and sets us to the tasks which He has to fulfill for our time. He commands. And to those who obey Him, whether they be wise or simple, He will reveal Himself in the toils, the conflicts, the sufferings which they shall pass through in His fellowship, and, as an ineffable mystery, they shall learn in their own experience Who He is.[2]

Who is Jesus? The only way to answer this question is to come to know him. And we come to know him as we accept him into our hearts and make him the Lord of our lives. What Reza Aslan seems to have forgotten is that Jesus is not just some historical figure from the past; Jesus is a living presence now. And the more we come to know him, the closer we come to the Father who sent him, and who dwelt in him, and who gave him for us that we might have eternal life. John wrote: "No one has ever seen God. It is God the only Son, who is close to the Father's heart, who has made him known."

GRACE LIKE RAIN
(John 1:14-18)

One evening I was driving to Washington, D.C. to attend a meeting of the executive committee of the D.C. Baptist Convention. Just as I was merging onto Route 50, the sky opened, the rain started to fall, and the wind began to blow with a ferocity that thunderstorms can have. The rain was pouring down, and the wind was gusting so hard that I had to hold on to keep my car from zigzagging all over the road. By the time I reached the District, the storm had passed, and except for all the leaves strewn on the roadway, you would not know how severe the weather had been just a few minutes earlier.

Just then, a song came on the radio that I had never heard before, with the refrain, "Hallelujah, grace like rain falls down on me." Even though I had never heard the song, the lyrics were familiar because it was an adaptation of the hymn, "Amazing Grace." The tune was different, the refrain was new, and the style was more edgy than traditional church music.

When the song was finished, I pulled over to the side of the road so I could write down the name of the song and the recording artist. The next day I ordered the CD, *Grace Like Rain*, by Todd Agnew. I learned that Todd Agnew, at the time, was a 33-year-old Native American singer, songwriter, and worship leader. He had been adopted by a Christian family in Texas when he was an infant, and he was raised in the church, learning all the familiar hymns of the faith. As he grew older, Todd discovered that sometimes those old hymns can lose their meaning, because they are so familiar. So, he took the words to "Amazing Grace," added a new refrain, and set them to the folk-rock beat of contemporary Christian music, to allow those beloved old lyrics to have a new hearing.

Maybe you remember the story behind the original hymn, "Amazing Grace." It was written by an English pastor named John Newton, and his story is a tale of grace in itself. John Newton was born in London in 1725. His mother was a pious churchgoing woman, a dissenter from the Church of England who taught her son to memorize scripture and learn hymns by heart at an early age. She took young John to an Independent (Congregational) church, akin to the Puritan faith. When John was only seven, his mother died, and his life took a radical turn. His father was not a religious man. In fact, he was a sea captain, and at the age of 11, John began to accompany his father on a series of sea voyages. Back home, between voyages, his stepmother allowed John to do whatever he wanted, and he got into the kind of trouble one might expect an unsupervised and undisciplined teenage boy to get into.

During his sea voyages the adolescent John was exposed to a rough and vulgar way of life, along with the slave trade. At the age of 18, John Newton was forcibly conscripted into the Royal Navy by a press-gang. He became a crewman aboard a British man-o-war, enduring extreme hardships and dangers at sea. At the first opportunity, he tried to escape from the ship and run away from the Navy, but he was caught, arrested, dragged back to the ship in chains, and flogged with a cat-o-nine-tails. All these experiences served to harden a young man who had lost his mother as a child and had been exposed to inhumane conditions at sea. Over the next few years John Newton suffered illness, hunger, and near drowning when he fell overboard. Along the way, he lost whatever religious faith his mother had planted in him. He drank heavily, and he began swearing and blaspheming to such a degree that even the older, hardened sailors were shocked.

A turning point in Newton's life occurred when he was 23, during a slave-trading voyage from Brazil to Newfoundland. His ship was caught in a violent storm and one crewmember was swept away into the churning sea. Newton tied himself to the ship to keep from being washed overboard as well. During the long night, Newton began to think that the violent storm was punishment for his reprobate lifestyle. He feared that he was too great a sinner to have any hope of God's mercy and grace. But when the storm subsided, Newton concluded that God had delivered him for some purpose. Later he would write that this was "the hour I first believed."

John Newton's conversion did not take place all at once. Soon after the crisis had passed, he slid back into his sinful lifestyle. But months later, when he fell ill with a high fever, he came to himself once again and recommitted his life to God. Still, his transformation was not complete. Newton continued to be involved in the slave trade, even becoming captain of a slave ship. At that point, his religious conversion had not changed his attitude about slavery. He still accepted slave trading as an honorable profession. But in most other aspects of his life, John Newton was a changed man. He began to pray and read the Bible. Eventually he began praying for his slave cargo, and his increasing distaste for the slave trade led him to give up life at sea and accept a position as a tide surveyor in Liverpool. It was a well-paid government job that involved boarding vessels as they entered the harbor and inspecting them for smuggled goods.

Back home in England, John Newton began to act on his religious convictions. He became a protégé of the evangelist George Whitfield and began to follow him around on his preaching missions through the countryside. In Liverpool he attended small "religious societies" that met for preaching, prayer, and Bible study. On his own he began teaching himself Greek and Hebrew and studying "books of divinity." John Newton began to sense that God was calling him into the ministry.

After a seven-year struggle through the ordination process, Newton finally became an ordained minister in the Church of England. But many bishops were wary of Newton, both because of his checkered past, and because of his "enthusiast" leanings and association with the likes of Whitfield. Finally, he was appointed curate of a congregation in the English midlands village of Olney. There, John Newton relished his work as a pastor that included preaching, teaching, visiting, working with children of the parish, and hymn writing.

One of the hymns he wrote while pastor at Olney he titled, "Faith's Review and Expectation." We know it today as "Amazing Grace." The hymn was largely auto-biographical, reflecting Newton's inglorious past as a blaspheming sailor and later captain of a slave ship. He wrote, "Amazing grace, how sweet the sound, that saved a wretch like me." Newton considered himself a wretch, saved only by the amazing grace of God. In later years he referred to himself as "the old African blasphemer." He eventually became an outspoken opponent of the slave trade.

After becoming a pastor in London later in his life, Newton befriended a member of Parliament named William Wilberforce, who led the campaign to abolish the slave trade in England. Wilberforce even arranged for the aged Newton to testify before Parliament against the slave trade, as a former slave trader himself. Before he died in 1807, Newton wrote his own epitaph, which appears on his gravestone even today:

> John Newton, clerk, once an infidel and libertine,
> A servant of slaves in Africa, was,
> By the rich mercy of our Lord and Savior Jesus Christ,
> Preserved, restored, pardoned, and appointed
> To preach the faith that he had long laboured to destroy.

"Amazing Grace" was more than just a hymn that John Newton wrote. It became the theme of Newton's life. It is not too much to say that "amazing grace" is the theme of the Christian life too.[3]

In the scripture passage from the prologue to John's gospel, we read that "the Word became flesh and lived among us...full of grace and truth." John continued, "from his fullness we have all received, grace upon grace. The law indeed was given through Moses; grace and truth came through Jesus Christ."

Grace is the unmerited favor of God. Grace is God's attitude toward us, even though we are all sinners. Grace is God's mercy and forgiveness. Grace is the Word become flesh. Grace is the gift of God's Son. Grace is Jesus dying on the cross for our sins. Grace is the expression of God's love. John said that God sent his Son to offer us grace upon grace. God's grace falls on us like rain. That is what the Christian faith is all about, God loving us so much that he gave his only Son.

John Newton, the old blasphemer who captained a slave ship, came to understand that even a wretch like himself could receive God's grace. It did not happen all at once, but God's amazing grace began to change his life. He gave up slave trading and a life of wantonness and debauchery and became a preacher of the gospel. In fact, he became an ardent opponent of slave trading and an ardent defender of the Christian faith.

If a man like John Newton could be forgiven, pardoned, restored, and redeemed, then anyone can be saved. God wants to rain down his grace upon your life and wash your sins away. God wants to work a miracle of transformation and make you a new person too. The melody may change, but the message remains the same. As John Newton (and then Todd Agnew) put it:

> Amazing grace, how sweet the sound
> That saved a wretch like me
> I once was lost but now I'm found
> Was blind but now I see so clearly
>
> Hallelujah, grace like rain falls down on me
> Hallelujah, and all my stains are washed away,
> They're washed away

QUESTIONS FOR DISCUSSION/REFLECTION

1. What connections do you see between the beginning of John's gospel and the beginning of Genesis?
2. What is the meaning of the "Word" in John?
3. John 1:3 and 1:10 describe the role of the Word/Jesus in creation. Compare this understanding with 1 Corinthians 8:6, Colossians 1:16, and Hebrews 1:2.
4. How would you describe the relationship of the Son to the Father?
5. In what ways has the Son made the Father known?

NOTES

[1]Reza Aslan, *No god but God: The Origins, Evolution, and Future of Islam* (Random House, 2005), 7.

[2]Albert Schweitzer, *The Quest of the Historical Jesus* (Dover Publications, 2005), 403.

[3]"John Newton and the Story of Amazing Grace," *Christian History & Biography*, Winter 2004.

About the Author

Bruce Salmon served for 33 years as pastor of Village Baptist Church in Bowie, Maryland. During that time, he preached almost 1,500 original Sunday morning sermons, including about 140 sermons on the Christmas story. For the last 18 years of his ministry, he taught a Sunday morning pastor's class in which adults read and discussed entire books of the Bible. He also led winter, summer, and Lenten Sunday evening adult studies that covered various topics and Bible books, including the following:

- Introducing the New Testament
- The Sermon on the Mount
- The Life of Christ
- The Life of Paul
- The Passion of Jesus
- The Jesus of the Bible
- Genesis
- Exodus
- Joshua
- 1 Samuel
- 2 Samuel
- Isaiah
- Ezekiel
- Malachi
- Matthew
- Mark
- Luke
- John
- Acts
- Romans
- 2 Corinthians
- Hebrews
- James
- Revelation

A native of Fort Worth, Texas, Salmon received the Bachelor of Arts with a major in English from Baylor University and the Master of Divinity and Doctor of Ministry degrees from the Southern Baptist Theological Seminary. He also received the Master of Arts in Counseling Psychology from Bowie State University, with a specialization in Clinical Pastoral Counseling.

Salmon has served on several committees of the D.C. Baptist Convention and on several commissions of the Baptist World Alliance. In addition to this volume and others in the series *Spelunking Scripture*,* he is the author of *Storytelling in Preaching* (BSSB, 1988) and *Preaching for the Long Haul: A Case Study on Long-term Pastoral Ministry* (Nurturing Faith, 2019).

Salmon is husband to wife Linda, father to grown children Amy and Marc, father-in-law to Stacey, and grandfather to granddaughter Ford. In addition to studying the Bible, his interests include spectator sports, current events, music, museums, golf, and travel.

*For more information and blogs, visit www.spelunkingscripture.com.

CPSIA information can be obtained
at www.ICGtesting.com
Printed in the USA
BVHW041005100821
614083BV00016B/390